Have Bacteria Won?

Have Bacteria Won?

HUGH PENNINGTON

polity

The right of Hugh Pennington to be identified as Author of this Work has been asserted in accordance with the UK Copyright, Designs and Patents Act 1988.

First published in 2016 by Polity Press

Polity Press
65 Bridge Street
Cambridge CB2 1UR, UK

Polity Press
350 Main Street
Malden, MA 02148, USA

ISBN-13: 978-0-7456-9079-7
ISBN-13: 978-0-7456-9080-3 (pb)

A catalogue record for this book is available from the British Library.

Library of Congress Cataloging-in-Publication Data

Pennington, T. H. (Thomas Hugh)
   Have bacteria won? / Hugh Pennington.
     pages cm
   Includes bibliographical references.
   ISBN 978-0-7456-9079-7 (hardback) – ISBN 978-0-7456-9080-3
(pbk.) 1. Bacteria. 2. Viruses. 3. Communicable diseases–
Prevention. 4. Communicable diseases–Treatment. 5. World
health. 6. Epidemics–History. I. Title.
   QR75.P36 2015
   579.3–dc23

                                                    2015016898

Typeset in 11 on 15 pt Adobe Garamond
by Toppan Best-set Premedia Limited
Printed and bound in the United Kingdom by Clays Ltd, St Ives PLC

The publisher has used its best endeavours to ensure that the URLs for external websites referred to in this book are correct and active at the time of going to press. However, the publisher has no responsibility for the websites and can make no guarantee that a site will remain live or that the content is or will remain appropriate.

Every effort has been made to trace all copyright holders, but if any have been inadvertently overlooked the publisher will be pleased to include any necessary credits in any subsequent reprint or edition.

For further information on Polity, visit our website:
politybooks.com

CONTENTS

Have Bacteria Won? is a title intended to scare you and make you read on. 'Bacteria' conjures up an army of malevolent germs, and 'won' implies losing a war against them. Moreover, predictions abound of a return to the world of pre-Florence Nightingale horrors as we enter an apocalyptic post-antibiotic era. But are these fears justified? Let's start by putting bacteria in their proper place. Those that live on our skin and in our mouths, throats and intestines are known collectively as the microbiome. On a single person its cells outnumber those of humans 10-fold, and bacterial genes outnumber human genes 360-fold. For most of our lives our relationship with the members of the microbiome is happy and profitable. We feed them, and they help us digest our food, make vitamins for us and compete successfully against ill-intentioned invaders. Of the 10,000 bacterial species that inhabit us, those that can cause disease are a tiny fraction and in fact they usually stay silent.

As for winning wars, microbiologists sometimes use military metaphors in grant applications, and usually go along with them in press releases puffing their latest 'breakthroughs', but we don't stand at our laboratory benches shouting 'Let's fight the captains of the men of death' – although, to be fair, most of us don't regularly read John Bunyan, who described consumption (tuberculosis) thus in 1680.

Viruses are not bacteria. Unlike them, they can't make proteins on their own and so can't grow outside cells. Technically they are 'obligate intracellular parasites', which means that they need host genes and so can get by with far, far fewer of their own. But patients don't worry much about the taxonomy of the agent that is causing their illness. So viruses – and other microbes – get full coverage in this book. Ebola is a virus, for example, but the rhetoric used in relation to it is just the same as that deployed over bacteria.

A former US Surgeon General, William Stewart, is still quoted as saying: 'It is time to close the books on infectious diseases, and declare the war on pestilence won.' It should be made clear that Stewart never uttered these words – he is alleged to have made them in a presentation, some say it was given in 1967, and others that it was in 1969, but the notes of his speeches do not contain them. In fact the records show that he said the opposite. At the 1967 Meeting of the Association of State and Territorial Health Officers, when he was supposed to have called time on infectious diseases, he stated that 'warning flags are still flying in the communicable diseases field'. However, Stewart's words are used often, but always ironically, because antibiotics and vaccines have most certainly *not* 'won the war'. But does it therefore follow that the bacteria (and viruses) have won? There is no simple answer, because each species has to be considered individually; their natural histories vary enormously. Some evolve during a single infection in a single patient; others change little over centuries. As hosts we also vary enormously from individual to individual, and change our behaviour and lifestyles, sometimes more rapidly than the microbes. Equally radical have been the changes in our attitudes to them, and to health, and to death.

The current situation is that despite many unanswered questions and much remaining ignorance, it is beyond dispute that big battles have been won on both sides – mostly on ours. But the struggle continues, aided by science for us, and evolution and our follies for them (bacteria/viruses), with our behaviour and our politics sometimes aiding one side, then the other. The nature of our intimate relationship with bacteria and viruses means that 'the war' will go on for ever.

There has been much antimicrobial progress: our infants are no longer carried off by diarrhoea as a matter of course; smallpox has joined the dodo in extinction in nature; and poets, novelists and composers like Keats, the Brontës and Chopin no longer are carried off prematurely by consumption. Pneumonia is still for many the 'old man's friend'; but it no longer commonly kills us in our prime. Nevertheless, we are still very afraid of the microbes. Chapter 1 considers why this is the case. Chapter 2 brings the good news: how reductions in biodiversity have been delivered, why this has been beneficial for us – and demonstrates the important fact that not all the antimicrobial benefits have been due to deliberate design, but have been accidental by-products. Chapter 3 brings the bad news: the appearance and spread of mutant clones and other nasty novelties. Chapter 4 shows how our actions (or inactions) help the microbes, and agrees with George Santayana's verdict on history that 'those who cannot remember the past are condemned to repeat it'. Chapter 5 is about politics: bacteria and viruses don't just kill people, but regularly misbehave by not following the predictions we make for them and destroy government departments and politicians' careers; politics sometimes destroys microbiologists as well.

Introduction

Case studies have great heuristic value. Using them is the best way to address the very big differences between the microbial species that harm us and the way we respond to them. The stories these chapters contain describe real events that often outdo fictional ones in terms of horror. But there are happy endings, too, as we shall see.

ONE

Why Are We So Worried About Bacteria?

The average life expectancy in industrialized countries has nearly doubled in the last 150 years. The pensions industry has a vested interest in understanding why, of course, and a report prepared by the Pensions Institute[1] in the UK was called *Apocalyptic Demography?* for good reason. While, on the negative side, it concluded that, 'since we have to die of something, it is most likely to be cancer for the foreseeable future', more positively it also pointed out that for the last 40 years 'UK life expectancy projections have consistently underestimated future mortality improvements'.

The age-standardized mortality rates in England and Wales in 2013 were 22% lower for men and 19% lower for women than in 2003. The *Office for National Statistics Bulletin* for that year reported that cancers accounted for 29% of all deaths, while circulatory diseases (which include deaths from ischaemic heart disease and strokes) and respiratory diseases (including deaths from pneumonia, mostly in the old) accounted for 28%

and 15% of deaths, respectively. At the beginning of the twentieth century there was another disease group with a high mortality rate: infections. By 2013, however, this group no longer merited a comment. As a cause of death it ranked above cancers until the early 1920s, when infection death rates started to fall from the higher levels during World War I. With the exception of a blip at the beginning of World War II, the decline was relentless. It was the same in all rich countries; in 2013 30.6% of US citizens died from major cardiovascular diseases, 22.5% from cancer, but only 4.9% from infections. Most of the reduction and the biggest rate of decline happened before the introduction of antibiotics. But infections and their causes still rank high as things to fear. Why?

There is no simple answer. Fear is widespread. As Mary Douglas and Aaron Wildavsky[2] wryly remarked: 'What are Americans afraid of? Nothing much, really, except the food they eat, the water they drink, the air they breathe, the land they live on, and the energy they use.' Who is to blame for engendering so much fear? Is it the media? Can experts, or the government, or anyone else be trusted to tell the truth? Why have some infections been demonized? Are we worried about the right ones? The case studies that follow illustrate and consider these questions.

BSE/CJD

The idea that eating beef could give you dementia made many Britons very afraid in the 1990s. It is a good place to start the 'battlefield' analysis, not only because of the fear engendered by bovine spongiform encephalopathy (popularly known as 'mad cow disease'), but because it illustrates that this book uses 'bacteria' in a very broad sense; there are doubts about the exact nature of the agent that causes BSE, although all agree that it is neither a bacterium nor a virus.

The first reported case of BSE in the world[3,4] developed in a cow on a farm in Sussex. It started to show signs of illness in the summer of 1984. The disease was not caused by any known bacterium or virus. It was brand new. More cases occurred in English cows, and in 1987 a scientific paper was published describing it as similar to scrapie, a chronic transmissible brain disease in sheep. By this time there had been about 150 cases. There was evidence that the disease was being spread by recycling: meat and bone meal from cattle was being fed to other cattle as a source of protein. This practice was banned in May 1988, and in June of that year meat from animals sick with BSE was prohibited from entering the human food chain. The carcasses of sick animals were incinerated. In November 1989 the

Bovine Offal (Prohibition) Regulations came into force, stopping the entry of 'risk offals', particularly brain and spinal cord, into the food chain. Advisory committees were established by the UK government, and in 1990 the CJD Surveillance Unit in Edinburgh started work. CJD, a human brain disease with links to BSE in cows, is named after the German neuropathologists Hans Creutzfeld and Alfons Jakob, who described the illness in the 1920s. Its brain pathology is similar to that of scrapie. Typically, rapidly progressive dementia occurs in the late middle-aged. In 1995 several CJD cases in young people were referred to the Unit. This was bad news, because hitherto CJD in the young had been very rare. And the brain histopathology of some of the cases – the appearance of brain tissue under the microscope – was novel, being different from that in the small number of cases that had occurred in the young before. In March 1996 the definite conclusion was reached that these CJD cases were caused by exposure to BSE. The condition was called variant CJD (vCJD). The epidemic started in 1994, when eight people fell ill in the UK. The first deaths (three) happened in 1995. vCJD peaked in 2000 with 27 diagnoses and 28 deaths. There were no deaths in 2012 and only one in 2013. No diagnoses have been made since, and no cases have been diagnosed in people born after 1989. Four people were infected by blood transfusions in 1999 or earlier from apparently healthy individuals who later developed vCJD. The total number of deaths from vCJD in the UK is 177, with a median age at death of 28.

In February 1996 the official government line was that British beef was safe to eat. A Ministry of Agriculture, Fisheries and Food leaflet was prepared by officials at the end of the month declaring that 'There is currently no scientific evidence to indicate a link between BSE and CJD' and that 'The independent expert committee set up to advise the government on all aspects of BSE is satisfied that British beef is safe to eat.' It went to Ministers in March for approval, but was overtaken by events. The public announcement of a link in the House of Commons on the afternoon of 20 March was nicely summarized in advance by the tabloid paper, *The Mirror*, when it reported the news that had been leaked that morning: 'Official: Mad cow can kill you'.

Why was there so much confidence that beef was safe until just before the early evidence became strong – even if still circumstantial – that BSE and vCJD were linked? The first hypothesis had been that BSE was caused by the scrapie agent. For 200 years, individuals had been eating mutton from infected animals without coming to any harm. When the scrapie hypothesis was shown to be unlikely, it was still believed that because

BSE had the same properties, it would behave in the same way. It was considered very unlikely that it would cross the species barrier from cattle to humans, or that it would be infectious by mouth. And had not a range of control measures been put in place on a precautionary basis that would protect the public even if these guesses were wrong?

What we got wrong at the very beginning of BSE was thinking that it was just scrapie in cattle, and we made the mistake of thinking that even if it was not, it would still behave in the same way. Even so, the control measures seem to have worked, in that nobody born after the implementation of the ban of brains and spinal cords from entering the food chain in 1989 has developed vCJD.

The main result of years of intensive studies on vCJD and BSE is the expansion of our areas of ignorance. We still cannot explain why nearly all the human victims were young. Although it is reasonable to assume that millions were exposed to meat products containing the BSE agent, neither can we explain why so few came down with vCJD.

Scrapied sheep scratch, have a tremor and fall over. The disease is very contagious, but the precise details as to how it spreads are still uncertain. Its incubation period is very long. The infectious agent is neither a bacterium nor a virus. It is resistant to heat and radiation and chemicals like formaldehyde. Stanley Prusiner proposed in 1982 that it was a 'novel infectious agent', which he called a 'prion', and considered it to be a protein. He won the Nobel Prize for his work. There is no doubt that the protein he identified, PrP, plays a central role in diseases like scrapie, BSE and vCJD. In humans it is coded for by a gene on chromosome 20, termed PNRP. More than 40 mutations in it have been found. Some are associated with CJD. But some, myself included, have doubts that the prion protein alone is the infectious agent.[3]

Everyone got BSE/vCJD wrong. The pessimists – 'a generation is doomed' – were far too pessimistic, and the optimists far too optimistic. So the public was right to be scared. The science of BSE/CJD still remains very uncertain. It is far less so for the causes of our next fearful and frightful entity.

Necrotizing fasciitis

Many of us will have heard of the flesh-eating bug, the cause of necrotizing fasciitis. Foundations have been established to help its victims and the relatives of those who have died of it. Atul Gawande devoted the last chapter in his 2002 best-seller *Complications* to it. In necrotizing fasciitis (NF), bacteria digest and destroy tissues just under the skin. Most victims are healthy. It starts without warning, spreads very fast and is often fatal; for survivors, plastic surgery is often needed to cover the gaping hole that is left. It was first described in China in 1924 by Frank L. Meleney, an American surgeon working at the Peking Union Medical College.[5] Its nature remains the same today as when he described it. Also unchanged are its treatment – vigorous and generous surgery to cut out the infection – and its results. Meleney's success rate was much the same as those achieved today. But NF is very rare. It wasn't mentioned in the 1,389-page surgery textbook I used as a medical student in the 1950s. Its rise to prominence in the UK was caused by the media.

An apparent cluster of cases occurred in the UK in Gloucestershire in February, April and early May 1998, when they were reported by a local radio station. The Press Association picked up the story on 11 May, and it was run by the *Daily Sport* two days later. This paper specialized in softcore pornography and celebrity stories; its headline was 'BUG THAT EATS YOU ALIVE' and in lower case, 'Killer virus scoffs three', bouncing its traditional busty blonde to a side bar. After a 10-day lag period the story took off in the national press. Two days later it spread to TV and radio. Coverage continued for nearly a week. It ended abruptly in the electronic media on 28 May when the strength of the story about an attack on street begging by the then UK Prime Minister, John Major, killed it off. Coverage concluded with leaders in the medical and scientific weekly journals, the *Lancet*, the *British Medical Journal*, *Nature* and *Science*.

The NF story spread in the same way as if the story itself had been caused by a bacterium or a virus.[6] The radio report was the initial inoculation. The picking up of the story by the Press Association and its dissemination before mass publication was the incubation period, a silent time when the microbe is quietly multiplying in the body but has not yet caused symptoms. The initial breaking of the story in the *Daily Sport* resembled the prodromal period, when the sufferer starts to feel unwell but doesn't yet have diarrhoea, or a rash, or excruciating pain or a raging fever. The appearance of the story in the print media signalled the full-blown infection, and the promulgation by radio and TV which followed was like the spread of an infection from the bowels or the lungs or the bladder via the bloodstream to deeper organs like the kidneys, the bones or the brain.

In essence, nothing new happened in 1998, except that journalists had got hold of a good human interest story: a bacterium that struck at random out of the blue (it could be you next!), that killed in a horrible way, but left enough survivors keen to tell their powerful stories with punch lines that were a gift to subeditors – 'Her flesh was being eaten away. Only one thing stood between Helen and Death... Thank God I'M FAT' (*Take a Break*) – and to take part in a detailed TV documentary about some of the Gloucestershire cases.

The way this story was presented made it into an outbreak. NF was a new condition for journalists and for the public. Cases seemed easy to find. But there was no epidemiological link between most of them; they occurred randomly. The outbreak was not of infection, but of media interest. And the coverage engendered much public concern.

Dionysius Lardner described this process well:[7]

In the modes of travelling used before the prevalence of railways, accidents to life and limb were frequent, but in general they were individually so unimportant as not to attract notice, or find a place in the public journals. In the case of railways, however, where large numbers are carried in the same train, and simultaneously exposed to danger, accidents, though more rare, are sometimes attended with appalling results. Much notice is therefore drawn to them. They are commented on in the journals, and public alarm is excited.

Outbreaks of infection have the same impact as rail crashes. When they are handled poorly, the analogy is perfect.

Typhoid in Aberdeen

A classic example of misfortune in this regard is the Aberdeen typhoid outbreak in May and June 1964, caused by contaminated Argentinian corned beef.[8] Eating it caused 50 cases, many in young women in the prosperous West End of the city who were consuming it as part of a slimming diet. Cross-contamination of other meats from a slicing machine and knives was responsible for another 450. The local joke 'Only in Aberdeen could you get 500 slices out of a can of corned beef' still gets a laugh. But there was no humour at the time. The Aberdeen Medical Officer of Health, Dr Ian MacQueen, had fallen out with the local bacteriologist. Dr MacQueen's knowledge of the natural history of typhoid fever was defective. He knew even less about the bacterium itself. He became obsessed with the notion that the outbreak would assume enormous proportions because of person-to-person spread and spread from carriers. He said that 40,000 people were at risk. To prevent a 'second wave' of cases, he mounted a vigorous publicity campaign, appearing nightly on television. Before training in medicine he had had journalistic aspirations, but became a doctor because of better employment prospects. Even so, the reporters with whom he dealt considered his handling of the press to be naïve. One said, 'You could feed him a line ... "Is it fair, then, Dr MacQueen, to call this a beleaguered city?" ... and of course he said "Yes".' So Aberdeen became known as the 'Beleaguered City'. Crazy things were done. The University of Aberdeen put out 'Typhoid Notices'. Number 3 on 3 June said: 'There is a remote risk of infection from perspiration on examination scripts. Examiners who wish to take precautions on this score should wear cotton gloves.' The three city ballrooms were closed. Children were not allowed to go to cinemas unaccompanied. The publicity had an international impact. There was a rumour in the US that bodies had been piled on the beach waiting for burial. Cattle raisers in Paraguay, Kenya and Tanzania suffered economic loss. But no cases caused by spread from a sufferer or a carrier were identified, only five cases continued to excrete the organism a year after the outbreak, and nobody died directly from the infection.

From time to time the media behave like a cheap refracting telescope, focusing on an object of interest but magnifying it with a good deal of aberration and fuzziness at the edges because of the poor quality of their lenses. This is why public statements by those trying to control an outbreak have to be handled with a lot more care than they were in Aberdeen. Outbreaks bring bacteria and viruses to public attention and engender fear. Even the names of certain diseases and microbes are enough to spread panic.

Leprosy, Ebola and MRSA

Leprosy has engendered fear for more than a millennium. Today it would be considered offensive to call someone with leprosy a leper, because of its modern meaning having entered our language as a synonym for 'outcast'. Maybe that is why in the US it is now called Hansen's disease. On a positive note, the historical prominence of leprosy meant that *Mycobacterium leprae*, the causative organism, was the first bacterium to be unequivocally linked to an infection. Armauer Hansen demonstrated it in samples taken from a patient in his leprosy hospital in Bergen in 1873, though nearly 200 years of scientific study has failed to answer hardly any of the old questions about leprosy and indeed set new puzzling ones: How is infection transmitted? Why is it that the nine-banded armadillo is the only animal – apart from the human – that develops leprosy?

Perhaps surprisingly, leprosy is not particularly contagious or rapidly fatal. Most people do not develop the disease when exposed to the bacterium. They have an innate resistance to it. But its victims have experienced very real ostracism for centuries, owing to the very visible effects it produces on the face and the hands. So it is safe to conclude that the reputation of a particular disease, however longstanding and however firmly held, can be very misleading. It is the same today with the communicability of Ebola fever (both those infected by and exposed to it being honorary 'lepers'), as one recent international story shows.

When Kaci Hickox flew into Newark Liberty International Airport in New Jersey on 24 October 2014, she was taken to the University Hospital in Newark and put into an isolation tent. She had just come back from Sierra Leone, where she had been working with Médecins Sans Frontières looking after Ebola victims.

A forehead scanner at the airport registered a temperature of 101°. She had not had a fever earlier that day, and she didn't have one later. She tested negative for the virus. She was annoyed by the restrictions, and after negotiations between her lawyers and the State Attorney General's office, she was allowed to drive to her home in Maine four days later. Maine requested that she remain quarantined in her house and petitioned the Fort Kent District Court to that effect. Judge LaVerdiere disagreed.[9] He ordered that she (the Respondent) be monitored daily. He went on to make some very wise remarks:

> The Court pauses to make a few critical observations. First, we would not be here today unless Respondent generously, kindly and with compassion lent her skills to aid, comfort, and care for individuals stricken with a terrible disease. We need to remember as we go through this matter that we owe her and all professionals who give themselves in this way a debt of gratitude. Having said that, Respondent should understand that the court is fully aware of the misconceptions, misinformation, bad science and bad information being spread from shore to shore in our country with respect to Ebola. The Court is fully aware that people are acting out of fear and that this fear is not entirely

rational. However, whether that fear is rational or not, it is present and it is real. Respondent's actions at this point, as a health care professional, need to demonstrate her full understanding of human nature and the real fear that exists. She should guide herself accordingly.

Her monitoring finished on 10 November. She never showed signs of the disease.

Acronyms like CJD and HIV can be even better at engendering fear than a name. Since 1997, MRSA, the methicillin-resistant *Staphylococcus aureus*, has been called a 'killer superbug' by the tabloid press and a 'potentially fatal superbug' by the broadsheets.[10] It has the same reputation in the US. In the UK it became a big party political issue in 2004, and many human interest stories were published in the run-up to the UK General Election in May 2005. I am regularly formally instructed by lawyers to write medico-legal expert witness reports. Since 2010 I have prepared 80 on patients treated in hospital for infections, of which 54 have been on those infected or carrying *Staphylococcus aureus*, 31 with MRSA, and 23 with methicillin-sensitive (MSSA) strains. The number of patients is small, but in preparing the reports I have seen all the hospital records, witness statements by the patients and often their close relatives, and the opinions of other experts. This work provides strong evidence about how MRSA is perceived not only by patients, but also by the lawyers they have consulted.

Eleven patients who wanted to sue because they had had MRSA had no physical symptoms caused by the organism; they were carriers only. Another 11 had local infections after surgery, all treated successfully. One patient developed a spinal abscess, and one had an amputation because an arterial graft had become infected. Three had died from their MRSA infections: one from septicaemia, one from pneumonia and one from the bursting of an infected major blood vessel.

In contrast, none of those infected with MSSA were just carriers; in five the infection had led to amputation, four had spinal infections (one fatal and two resulting in paraplegia), two had septic shock (one fatal), five had joint infections requiring further surgery, two had breast infections needing further surgery, one had had necrotizing fasciitis after a caesarian section, one developed osteomyelitis of the femur requiring complicated surgery, and one had an infection of his scrotum with much tissue damage.

The consensus view of bacteriologists is that MRSA infections are no more severe than those caused by

MSSA. Both can be lethal or life changing, and both organisms can be carried without causing disease. But my medico-legal experience shows that MRSA engenders much fear as an acronym alone. So as fear factors, the names of microbes and of the diseases they cause are lead actors – folk memories give them longevity. The list of notifiable diseases in the UK (i.e. any disease required by law to be reported to the authorities) is a good guide to dramatic events and diseases stigmatized long ago, as well as to our current worries. Leprosy is there, along with plague, cholera and typhus. So they are in the US, except that leprosy (as noted above) is called Hansen's disease and typhus 'spotted fever rickettsiosis'. But all the currently notifiable diseases combined kill by orders of magnitude fewer people in Britain today than one that isn't on the list, pneumonia, which every year carries off more women than breast cancer and more men than prostate cancer. The commonest cause is *Streptococcus pneumoniae*, the pneumococcus. Perhaps the reason it is not on the list is that it does not cause dramatic outbreaks in the UK, and so it doesn't hit the headlines.

Nevertheless, fear of MRSA brought benefits; public and political pressure has speeded up the introduction of evidence-based control measures in the US and the UK, countries which had underestimated its ability to spread in hospitals and from hospital to hospital. Sometimes the journalistic telescope finds hidden things that should be made public. A staff member of the *Dumbarton and Vale of Leven Reporter* did that in 2008, and uncovered bacteriological horrors at the Vale of Leven Hospital in Alexandria, Dumbartonshire.

Clostridium difficile, Alexandria

One of my daughters was born at the Vale in the 1970s. Situated not far south of the Scottish Highland line, with a superb view of Ben Lomond from the labour ward, the hospital, luckily, had not yet fallen on hard times, but by the beginning of this century it was in decline. It was the first to be built in Scotland after the establishment of the NHS. It opened in 1955 and provided a comprehensive local service. But by 2000 it was perceived to be too small to provide the specialist functions required of a twenty-first-century district general hospital. They were being transferred elsewhere; by 2004, surgery, maternity and accident and emergency had gone. Maintenance of the hospital was poor; wash hand basins had been bought to replace old cracked ones, but no money had been allocated to install them. The resident consultant microbiologist resigned in 2002 and was not replaced. Senior infection control doctors were based in distant hospitals. The scene was set for scandal.[11] Between January 2007 and June 2008 a series of *Clostridium difficile* (or *C. difficile*) outbreaks took place at the hospital, infecting 131 patients, with the bacterium being the underlying cause, or contributory factor, in 28 deaths. *C. difficile* is a bacterium that lives in the bowels. Some people carry it without coming to any harm. But it can destroy the intestines of the elderly, with lethal consequences, particularly in those in hospital who have been treated with broad-spectrum antibiotics. Because of ignorance, incompetence, a dysfunctional outbreak control team, an inadequate reporting system and failing committee structures, all these outbreaks went unnoticed. But on 5 June 2008 the local newspaper, the *Dumbarton and Vale of Leven Reporter*, asked how many *C. difficile* cases and fatalities had occurred in the previous six months. Answering the question initiated the process that should have started 18 months earlier. An outbreak control team was established. It met for the first time on 10 June.

We are right to be worried, not about being carried off in our prime, but about dying an undignified death with severe abdominal pain and explosive diarrhoea in a bed soaked with liquid faeces. Cholera and dysentery caused such things in Scutari (modern-day Üsküdar in Istanbul) in the 1850s, but Florence Nightingale was powerless to prevent them, though she attended to the sufferers' dignity. Both tasks were in the power of those running the Vale of Leven Hospital in Scotland 150 years later. But they failed miserably.

The *C. difficile* sufferers at the Vale of Leven Hospital were the victims of modern medicine. Many had been prescribed one of the 4 Cs, the *C. difficile*-predisposing antibiotics (cephalosporins, co-amoxiclav, clindamycin and ciprofloxacin), before they developed diarrhoea. Media investigation and coverage played an entirely beneficial role throughout the Vale of Leven scandal.

So worries about bacteria are not unfounded. The problem is that most of the time, aided often by unin-formed media coverage driven by sensationalism and focusing on 'human interest' stories, we worry about the wrong ones. But that is typical of most of our risk assessments. And the Thomas theorem – 'if men define situations as real, they are real in their consequences' – is as relevant today as when it was first postulated in 1928. Judge LaVerdiere in Maine in 2014 followed its precept. Nevertheless, justifiable fear can bring benefits.

In England the incidence of gonorrhoea fell very rapidly in the late 1980s, from an all-time peak in 1974 to an all-time low in 1993. The dramatic fall coincided perfectly with the appearance of AIDS in mainstream media reporting and public health campaigns around safer sex, particularly in the gay community. In chapter 2, we will remain on this positive note and examine more of our victories in the battle against infection.

TWO

Victories

Our fear of microbes belies the many successes we have had in waging battle against them. Different microbes have fallen to different modes of attack: drugs, vaccines, clean water, heat and dietary boosts to immunity. These will be illustrated in the case studies that follow.

We begin with the successful attack on smallpox. The chapter then considers the first deliberately designed and dramatically successful therapeutic anti-infection interventions, the use of antibodies against diphtheria, and of drugs against syphilis. These successes had an enormous influence in driving the science and practical application of bacteriology and immunology. The chapter proceeds to look at improvements in water supply, milk quality and diet; developments that brought major reductions in infection, but were not introduced with that intention. Their massive health benefits were unintentional by-products. And, as we will see, sometimes microbes surprise us, leading to innovative new ways to eradicate the diseases they can cause.

Smallpox

Smallpox has gone.[12] It is extinct in the wild. Evidence-based control attempts started with variolation, the deliberate infection of individuals with smallpox. Descriptions of its application in China by the blowing of powdered scabs into the nasal cavity had appeared in Chinese medical texts as early as the eleventh century. It was not until the eighteenth century, however, that the practice was applied in Britain and North America. Here the credit is given respectively to Lady Mary Wortley Montagu and to the Reverend Cotton Mather, who had learned about it from his slaves. Lady Mary's advocacy and Mather's declaration that it was not against Puritan principles stimulated its introduction on both sides of the Atlantic in 1721. Variolation prepared the way for vaccination. Edward Jenner's inquiries into the protective effect of a cowpox infection and his demonstration that inoculation with it made the subjects resistant to variolation were described in his 1798 treatise, *An Inquiry into the Causes and Effects of the Variolae Vacciniae, a Disease Discovered in Some of the Western Counties of England, Particularly Gloucestershire, and Known by the Name of the Cow Pox.* The international adoption of vaccination was immediate. The number of cases of smallpox fell in many countries. Infant vaccination became routine. But implementation was imperfect, and anti-vaccination pressure groups emerged, like the London Society for the Abolition of Compulsory Vaccination. Isolation of patients was a traditional control measure. But only when it became systematic did case numbers fall substantially. In London until 1886 (when the city's non-hospitalized smallpox cases were isolated for the first time in hospital ships and riverside encampments), they were nearly always in the hundreds, with much bigger outbreaks every four or five years; but in 1886 there were 24 fatal cases, in 1887 and in 1888 there were nine, and in 1889 there were none.

Although smallpox ceased to be endemic (naturally occurring and not imported) in the UK in 1934 and the US in 1949, it still posed a threat elsewhere in the world. In 1959 the World Health Organization began a programme to eradicate smallpox globally. By 1973 it remained endemic in only five countries: Bangladesh, India, Nepal, Pakistan and Ethiopia. In 1975, *Variola major* (case fatality rate 20% or more) had gone, but *Variola minor* (case fatality rate 1% or less) continued to circulate in Ethiopia, where a civil war was in progress. It persisted in Ogaden desert nomads and in villages where variolators (i.e. deliberate infection with small-pox in the manner of Lady Mary Wortley Montagu) were still active. Helicopters and fixed-wing aircraft were used in a vigorous search for cases of the disease. The last Ethiopian case, three-year-old Amina Salat, fell ill on 9 August 1976. She had been variolated. A press conference was organized and TV crews flew in. It was thought that she was the last case ever. But the virus had spread quietly to Somalia. Case searchers had to use Land Rovers with 10-ply tyres to prevent punctures from thorn scrub, and patients were paid to go into isolation in lean-to shelters surrounded by a *haro*, a barrier of thorn bushes that kept out animals and visitors. The last case, Ali Maow Maalin, fell ill on 22 October 1977 in Merca, but recovered quickly. That was the end of smallpox in the wild.

Its big weak spot had been its very close relationship to cowpox, meaning that a local skin infection with the latter produced strong immunity against it. The vaccine was simple and cheap to make by growing it in the skin of calves, it stayed alive in the heat when freeze-dried, and it was easily and effectively administered by a single skin scratch made by a forked needle. The rash made cases easy to spot, and diagnosis could be done in the field. Carriers did not exist, and there was no animal reservoir of infection. And of all the viruses that regularly infect humans, it had the lowest R_0 number. This is the basic reproduction rate, the average number of secondary infections produced by one infected person. The number for smallpox was low enough to mean that even if only 20% of a population were unvaccinated, the virus would still die out, because it would be unable to find enough susceptible individuals to keep going. Smallpox had played into our hands.

Diphtheria and syphilis

The last two decades of the nineteenth century and the first of the twentieth were golden times for the new science of bacteriology. Some bacteriologists did very well too. Emil von Behring was appointed *Geheimrat* (privy councillor) by Kaiser Wilhelm II with the title of *Exzellenz*, was raised to the nobility, had a villa on Capri, and in 1901 was the first recipient of the Nobel Prize for Medicine or Physiology, for 'his work on serum therapy, especially its application against diphtheria'.

Diphtheria had played into Behring's hands. Its mode of attack, a protein toxin, was its weakness. The toxin molecule has three domains. One binds to the cell surface, one facilitates its entry into the cell, and after entry the third domain lethally switches off protein synthesis and stimulates apoptosis, a suicidal process started by cell damage. Antibodies against the toxin neutralize it. Behring made them in animals. There is no evidence to support the legend that the first successful use was on a child in Berlin on Christmas night, 1891, but its administration in cases soon became widespread. In principle it is still used today, in exactly the same way. For maximum effectiveness, it has to be given without delay. If a doctor thinks that diphtheria is a possible diagnosis but is slow to obtain and administer the antiserum, a medical negligence case may well follow; the toxin can kill by damaging the heart.

The experimental use of whole blood or plasma from patients who have recovered from Ebola is also based on the principle that antibodies neutralize; in this case the virus itself, rather than a toxin.

The diphtheria vaccine is a toxoid: that is, the toxin has been chemically modified to become non-toxic but retain its immunogenicity. Rather than treating an established infection with antibodies, it stimulates their production and protects against it; active rather than passive immunity. Behring used toxin combined with antitoxin antibodies. Toxoid came in the 1920s. In England and Wales its uptake was slow. The diphtheria death rate fell gradually, with ups and downs, from 300 to 150 per million during the 40 years from 1901; general immunization with toxoid started at the end of 1940, and the fall in the death rate was precipitous. In 1951 it was 0.73 per million, and in 1959 it was zero.

Key to Behring's success against diphtheria was the manufacture of high-quality standardized antibodies. Paul Ehrlich, who worked out how to do this, was awarded the Nobel Prize in 1908 for his immunological research, although he realized that some infections resist immunological attack, and that only specific drugs would cure them. Syphilis was the first to fall. Ehrlich used what the Americans call the Edisonian approach – choosing an approach that built on what he already knew, so turning a wild goose chase into a fox hunt, but still trying one thing after another. The cause of syphilis, *Treponema pallidum*, was discovered in Berlin in 1905 by Fritz Schaudinn and Paul Hoffmann. Schaudinn was an expert on protozoa and classified the *Treponema* as such. Ehrlich was synthesizing organic arsenical compounds to treat protozoal infections, and so tried them against syphilis. His 606th compound worked. Salvarsan was introduced into clinical practice in 1911. It was toxic and had to be given by intravenous injection. Alexander Fleming was particularly good at administering it and made much money by treating the rich. Maybe this also explains his honorary membership of the Chelsea Arts Club.

Salvarsan was revolutionary, but it was not cheap. Earle Moore, the premier US syphilologist, said in his 1933 textbook *The Modern Treatment of Syphilis*:[13]

> Most individuals contract syphilis when they are young, at a time when their earning capacity is at a minimum. As soon as the diagnosis is made, advice is given as to treatment which may be as impossible of fulfilment as the advice to the tuberculous pauper to transplant himself from Maine to Arizona, to take a dozen eggs, a quart of cream, and a toddy of sherry daily.

But putting off treatment for syphilis was disastrous for many. Salvarsan only worked in the early stages of infection. The later manifestations of infection didn't show themselves for a decade or more. They were the complications that disabled and killed. Consider Frederick Delius, the British composer. According to Thomas Beecham, he had a 'decided preference for low life'. He lived in Paris from 1888 to 1896, moving in the Montparnasse circle with people like Paul Gauguin, August Strindberg, Alphonse Mucha, Edvard Munch, and Édouard Marchand, the *maître de ballet* of the Folies-Bergère. He fell ill in 1910, and over the next 15 years developed numbness in his hands, blurred vision and an unsteady gait. In 1925 his condition suddenly worsened. He went blind, lost the ability to sense his position in space and developed excruciating 'lightning pains' in his legs. He died nine years later. He had developed *tabes dorsalis*; *Treponema* had destroyed the nerve cells in and close to the spinal cord that transmit signals from muscles, joints and other tissues, telling the brain where they are. It had also killed his optic nerves. Delius was lucky. He went on composing; the *Treponema* had invaded his nervous system, but it had not damaged his frontal lobes. When it does, it causes the condition known historically as GPI, general paralysis of the insane, which has been Americanized and sanitized today to 'general paresis'. In its first stage and in its most dramatic form the sufferer exhibits exaggerated hyperbolic exaltation. A 1914 textbook[14] says:

The patient owns millions and millions; he is thousands of years old; he has hundreds of wives ... he will give cheques for millions, written on dirty bits of newspaper, to all bystanders ... [but] with all his grandeur and majesty ... he is easily influenced ... sent to an asylum he accepts the situation without murmur. His pupils are unequal. His speech is 'thick'. There is a tremor of the tongue.

In its second stage, fits start, and dementia gets worse. In the third stage, paralysis and dementia become complete, and the patient dies. As the big 1910 six-volume textbook *System of Syphilis* said, there is 'nothing more pitiable or degrading than the sight of these wrecks of humanity sitting in a row, their heads on their breasts, grinding the teeth, saliva running out of the angles of the mouth, oblivious to their surroundings, with expressionless faces and cold, livid, immobile hands'.[15]

Salvarsan had no effect on GPI, but there was another solution. *Treponema* in the brain hate heat. A high fever kills them. The Viennese psychiatrist Julius Wagner-Jauregg used malaria to induce it. Although the malaria in itself was lethal in a few cases, it cleared symptoms of GPI in about 25% of the remainder and alleviated them in 20%. In 1927 Wagner-Jauregg became the first doctor to receive the Nobel Prize for developing a new psychiatric therapy. To date only one other Nobelist has fallen into this category, Egas Moniz, in 1949, for showing the 'therapeutic value of leucotomy in certain psychoses'. Wagner-Jauregg's treatment remains the only example of the successful treatment of one infection with another. It made some mad men sane, and saved lives. But penicillin made it a historical curiosity. The *Treponema* is exquisitely sensitive. In the US the number of deaths from syphilis has fallen by more than 99% since its introduction. But nowhere has it been fully eradicated. In England in 2013 it was diagnosed in 2,970 men and 279 women. The ratio in the US was almost exactly the same: 15,861 cases to 1,500. The gender gap is not surprising because the immediate and short-term effects of infection are often clinically silent in women. The real surprise is how good the organism is at surviving, because it is as sensitive to penicillin as it was in the 1940s. It is our behaviours which allow it to survive. Serosorting, where men chose other men with the same HIV status as themselves for unprotected sex, and oral sex (thought to be relatively safe regarding HIV transmission, but a good way of transmitting syphilis) are helping it to survive. Nevertheless, as a threat to human health, it is a shadow of its former self, a curable condition not a potential death sentence.

Gas and water socialism, pasteurization

Diphtheria and syphilis were the first infections to be treated effectively by deliberate design. However, great successes in disease prevention have also arisen without any such conscious intent.

After taking advice in 1855 from Robert Stephenson and Isambard Kingdom Brunel, the city of Glasgow established a new water supply from Loch Katrine by building a 34-mile aqueduct, mostly in tunnels, to the city. It spared the city from cholera during the fourth pandemic in 1866. Only 68 died compared to 5,596 in London. But the main purpose of the Loch Katrine scheme was not the prevention of disease. Worries about cholera did not force its implementation,[16] the purpose of which was to supply water to a rapidly increasing population, help trade and fight fires; by 1864 the number of street fire hydrants had increased seven-fold.

Deaths from typhus fever in Glasgow fell from 3,607 in 1865–9 to 352 in 1875–9 and to 10 in 1906–10. Its mode of transmission was only established in 1909. Infected body lice shed *Rickettsia prowazekii*, its cause, in their faeces. Victims inoculate themselves by scratching the faeces into their skin. The louse lives in the seams of clothing; if clothes are regularly changed (more than once a month) and not slept in, the lice die of starvation and hypothermia. Glasgow started to establish municipal wash-houses – the 'steamies' – in the 1870s; in 1913 there were 979 stalls used by 821,329 wifies at 2d/hour. They made the big difference.

It was observed in 1903[17] that in Glasgow, a citizen

may live in a municipal house; he may walk along the municipal street, or ride on the municipal tramcar and watch the municipal dust cart collecting the refuse which is to be used to fertilise the municipal farm ... should he fall ill, he can ring up his doctor on his municipal telephone, or he may be taken to the municipal hospital in the municipal ambulance by a municipal policeman. Should he be so unfortunate as to get on fire, he will be put out by a municipal fireman using municipal water; after which he will, perhaps, forego the enjoyment of a municipal bath, though he may find it necessary to get a new suit in the municipal old clothes market.

This has been called 'gas and water socialism' and, in the US, 'sewer socialism', though this is perhaps something of a misnomer – in Milwaukee, the classic US example, socialists held power at the beginning of the twentieth century, but in Glasgow they did not. Nor should the power of business interests be ignored.

Pasteurization is another measure introduced for a good reason. It was also another urban improvement that had nothing to do with the prevention of disease (or socialist municipal benefit), but that was its unintended consequence.

In the 1860s, Louis Pasteur showed that exposing wine to a short burst of heat (up to 60°C) stopped it going sour. He demonstrated the same for beer. Milk was found to be subject to the same benefit and dairies started to pasteurize it with the sole purpose of prolonging its life. The first commercial pasteurizer was manufactured in Germany in 1880, and milk was being heat treated on a regular basis in Copenhagen and Stockholm by 1885. Milk pasteurization started in London at the beginning of the twentieth century and by 1939 93% of milk sold there was heat treated. During the first three decades of the twentieth century, there was an enormous fall in the number of cases of abdominal tuberculosis in the city's children. This was no coincidence – the disease is caused by the bovine tubercle bacillus. However, the percentage of pasteurized milk was much lower in the rest of England, particularly in small towns and in rural areas. Between 1912 and 1937, milk-borne outbreaks of infection were common in the UK: 113 outbreaks of scarlet fever, streptococcal sore throat, diphtheria, typhoid and paratyphoid fevers, dysentery and acute gastroenteritis were recorded. All were considered to have followed the consumption of raw unpasteurized milk or cream. In Scotland from 1970 to 1979, there were 29 *Salmonella* outbreaks affecting 2,500 raw milk drinkers. A big outbreak in Banffshire with two deaths was the stimulus for action. As ever, mortality drives policies to protect the health of the public. Pasteurization of all milk sold retail in Scotland became obligatory from 1 August 1983.[18]

To find good evidence that pasteurization of milk works well to protect the health of the public, one need only consider incidents that have happened because of technical failures in the process. A snowstorm in mid-January 1979 knocked out the electricity supply to a Scottish dairy supplying milk to consumers in South Kincardineshire and North Angus. The pasteurizer failed and the milk delivered on 15 January was raw. Two days later people started to fall ill with gastroenteritis. The cause was *Campylobacter*, a bacterium that is killed by pasteurization. There were 148 cases confirmed bacteriologically, and about 50% of those who drank the milk fell ill. In May 1994, a pasteurization failure caused milk supplied by the Redhouse Dairy in West Lothian to be contaminated with *E. coli* O157. There were 100 people infected. One child died and six developed renal failure and needed dialysis, two for the long term, with another receiving a kidney transplant. An economic analysis of the outbreak showed that it cost £3.2 million in the first year. Another *E. coli* O157 outbreak occurred in North Cumbria in early 1999. A poorly maintained pasteurizer was causing heat-treated milk to be contaminated with raw milk at the heat exchanger unit. In the following weeks 88 cases were reported, of whom 28 were hospitalized.

In England, Wales and Northern Ireland, raw unpasteurized milk can still be sold direct to consumers at the farm gate, through a farmhouse catering establishment or through milk roundsmen, farmers' markets and the internet. About 1% of the population is said to regularly consume it. There is pressure from lobby groups to relax the current regulations, and the Food Standards Agency debated the issue on 23 July 2014. The legal status of unpasteurized dairy products is also a political issue in the US. The law varies from state to state. A comparison of dairy product-associated disease outbreaks from 1993 to 2006 in different administrations showed a 150-fold greater incidence of outbreaks per unit consumed for unpasteurized products. Young people were affected in 60% of these outbreaks.[19] Drinking and eating unpasteurized products in rich countries is a choice usually made by people who can afford to eat whatever they like. It was not always so.

Diet

There is a pattern common to rich countries. The clinical effects of an infection become much less severe long before specific control measures or successful treatments become available. Their introduction then speeds up the decline, but from a low base. An adequate diet brings this about.

At the beginning of the twentieth century, the diet of most Glaswegians was inadequate. 'Wee bauchles' – stunted people bowlegged from rickets – were a characteristic sight in the city. Those who could barely afford milk would probably be getting it diluted with 'milk' from the 'iron cow' – the water pump. There was an enormous outbreak of measles in Glasgow in 1908 with 22,033 cases and 1,123 deaths. In children living in 'single ends' – one-room tenement flats – the mortality rate was 9.2% of those infected. For those living in flats and houses with four or more rooms it was 1.5%. It was the same at that time in Aberdeen; measles mortality was 6.8% in one-room dwellings and 0.8% in those with five of more rooms. Thus although measles was very common across the population in Glasgow and Aberdeen, in the bigger houses it was much less likely to be fatal. Better nutrition there was the main protector against death. General improvements in diet signalled the start of measles' transition from being a major killer to that of an unpleasant illness with occasional serious complications.

Tuberculosis is the other classic example. In England and Wales, mortality rates fell by 85% between the 1850s and 1940s, even though immunological surveys in the 1950s showed that nearly every middle-aged adult had been infected. Mortality rates fell by 89% between 1949 and 1959, after effective anti-tuberculosis drugs were introduced. Infection rates then started to fall as well. For tuberculosis, dietary improvement was crucial. The classic study demonstrating its importance was carried out by G.B. Leyton[20] at the prisoner of war hospital at Tost in Silesia (now Toszek, in Poland) – P.G. Wodehouse had been interned there in 1940 and 1941. Later in World War II it held 1,000 Russian and 250 British prisoners. The work regimes and holding conditions were the same for both nationalities; so was the food provided by the Germans. The rations were inadequate. They were calculated to provide only 1,611 calories per day. But the British received Red Cross food parcels, which provided another thousand calories. Chest X-rays showed lung lesions of tuberculosis in 1.2% of the British prisoners compared to 19% in the Russians, who tended to develop a rapidly progressive and fatal tuberculous bronchopneumonia.

There was a conspicuous exception, however, to the rule that infectious diseases become rarer as living standards improve. Over the course of the twentieth century, polio case numbers rose as infant death rates from all causes fell. The source of the virus is human faeces, and as virus circulation in communities diminished because hygiene improved, fewer children became infected. Infection in young children is less likely to cause paralysis, is most commonly silent, and leads to immunity. Fewer children becoming infected meant that as adults they lacked immunity, and now, unlike their ancestors, were susceptible to infection. The consequence of infection in *adults* is more severe. There was an outbreak of 106 cases of polio in British soldiers in Egypt in 1941 and 1942, when no polio was being reported elsewhere in the country. This was a great puzzle at the time – it was not understood that the virus could be circulating silently among young Egyptians. The outbreak went unreported because of censorship. This was a pity because it presaged what was to come, and was an example where mainstream reporting could have led to better outcomes. In England and Wales, the number of cases of acute paralytic polio increased 10-fold in 1947 and stayed high for the next decade. Polio vaccination was then introduced, and case numbers fell close to zero after another 10 years.

Surprises

Finding out 'new' information about microbes and disease – such as the silent circulation of the polio virus – can be greatly disconcerting, but information is an invaluable weapon, and can assist our battle in often surprising ways.

Wolbachia is one of the world's commonest parasitic microbes. It lives in insects and worms, its natural home being their reproductive systems. It takes feminism to extremes: it either kills males, or feminizes them, and being infected with it can enable sterile females to lay fertile eggs. Discovered in 1924, *Wolbachia* remained an entomological curiosity for 50 years, when its remarkable natural history began to be unravelled. Now it has its own website, and A-WOL, the Anti-Wolbachia Consortium, is funded by the Bill and Melinda Gates Foundation. What was the surprise that *Wolbachia* had in store for us?

Londoners who took refuge in the Underground during the Blitz were often attacked by ravenous mosquitoes. Medical entomologists love jargon and describe them as hypogeal, anthropophilic, autogenous, stenogamic and homodynamic: in other words underground-dwelling, human-biting, egg-laying without a previous blood meal, happy to mate in a confined space and breeding all year round.[21] Called *Culex pipiens* form *molestus*, they breed in puddles, flooded sumps and shafts in the Tube. They still attack maintenance workers. There is another urban *Culex pipiens* in London, form *pipiens*. It is ornithophilic (feeding only on birds), anautogenous (needing a blood meal before egg-laying), eurygamic (only mating in wide-open spaces), heterodynamic (hibernating in the winter) and epigeous (living on the surface). It breeds in water butts and garden ponds. So, like *molestus*, it is synanthropic – associated with humans.

If a mosquito-transmitted virus was introduced to London that had its natural home in birds and could infect humans as well, we would be safe because of the fastidious diets of the two forms of our native *Culex pipiens*. But that is not what happened in the US. Their two *Culex pipiens* forms have bred together. The hybrids bite both birds and humans. So when West Nile virus was introduced, it spread.[22] West Nile virus was discovered in 1937 in Uganda, and for many years it caused mild illnesses in Africa, Israel and France. It changed in the mid-1990s to become more virulent, with a minority of cases developing meningitis and encephalitis. In the US it first appeared in 1999: in New York, crows started to die in Queens and the Bronx. Human infections started two months later. Helped by bird migration, West Nile spread rapidly across the continent. In 2002 there were 4,156 cases and 284 deaths. It now occurs in every US state. The mosquitoes were the bridge vectors, transmitting the virus from birds to humans. The only good news was that there was no transmission from human to human, because the amount of virus in the blood of an infected person is too small to infect the mosquito, a necessary step for it to become a vector.

Could this happen in London? Possibly. But so far no hybrid mosquitoes have been found. It may well be that *Wolbachia* is responsible for this. *Culex pipiens* is infected with it, living in testis and ovary cells and doing no harm. Different populations of the mosquito have different *Wolbachia* strains. But only male and female mosquitoes with exactly the same *Wolbachia* strains can reproduce successfully. If they are different, embryo mortality is very high, sometimes 100%. It is very likely that form *pipiens* and form *molestus* in London have different *Wolbachia*. These bacteria are helping to keep Londoners safe, both from being bitten by mosquitoes from their garden water features, and from the viruses that they might transmit.

Wolbachia may be saving London, but it is making people blind in Africa and South America. Here this is not because it lives in a fly, but because it parasitizes a worm. Even so, its surprising symbiotic relationship with this worm offers us an exploitable weakness.[23]

Simulium is a fly whose larvae live in running water. It is a vicious biter and bloodsucker. The most notorious species in Europe is the Golubatz fly, taking its name from a castle on the Danube near the Iron Gates where it breeds, occasionally forming giant swarms big enough to kill cattle. The bite of *Simulium damnosum* and other species in Africa and South America spreads the round-worm, *Onchocerca volvulus*. Worm larvae mature and settle down under the skin to form nodules. Males migrate between the nodules to fertilize the females, which for the next decade release more than a thousand microfilariae – an early-stage form in the worm's devel-opmental life-cycle – every day. They are about 0.3 mm long and can live as long as two years. A heavily infected person will be inhabited with millions of them. A current estimate is that about 37 million people are infected with *Onchocerca*, most of them in Nigeria, Cameroon, Chad, Ethiopia, Uganda, Angola and the Democratic Republic of the Congo. *Simulium* flies are good vectors because when feeding they tear the skin and douse the wound with their anti-coagulant saliva to form a pool of blood. Each meal goes on for quite a long time, helped by the saliva having a local anaesthetic effect, making it more likely that they will ingest microfilariae, which also seem to be attracted to the bite site. The flies feed every few days, and have quite a long life, allowing the microfilariae they have sucked up to moult and become infectious at subsequent feeds.

Problems arise when the microfilariae die in the body of the host. There is a vigorous immune response by the infected person. It goes on for years. It causes severe itching and rashes at the beginning. The elasticity of the skin eventually gets damaged. It becomes thin and wrinkled. Microfilariae die in the cornea of the eye, and after years the victims eventually go blind; more than 250,000 people are currently estimated to be affected in this way.

Ivermectin treatment was introduced in 1987. This anti-worm drug was discovered by Merck, which donates 140 million treatments annually. A single dose controls the microfilariae for several months. However, even in the absence of re-infection the treatment has to be continued for at least 10 years, because ivermectin does not kill the adult worms. But the discovery that they have a symbiotic relationship with *Wolbachia*, which not only live in all individual worms at all life-cycle stages, but are necessary for the worms to grow and reproduce and have a long life, has made it possible to *cure* parasitized people by giving them six weeks of antibiotic treatment – targeting *Wolbachia* also deals with *Onchocerca*. And it is *Wolbachia* that seems to be the most important factor in the causation of skin disease and blindness, too, because it is the strong immune response triggered when the bacteria are released upon the death of the microfilariae that causes the damage to the skin and the cornea.

The unintended consequences of towns getting their water from the hills, milk pasteurization and better food have been enormous, and, at their best, vaccines and antibiotics have been brilliant successes. Expectations have been raised that in the fullness of time they will win the war. The British rear-guard fighting before Dunkirk in 1940 was over 'tetanus terrain': of the wounded soldiers who were evacuated, 16,000 had been vaccinated with the tetanus toxoid. None developed tetanus. Eight others did; they had all refused the immunization. But attempts to extend this kind of success to every kind of bacterial infection have failed. For years, Alexander Fleming was involved in the development of vaccines against *Staphylococcus aureus*, sore throats, gonorrhoea, rheumatism, ulcerative colitis and acne. But they were all useless.

So each microbe has to be considered separately. What works brilliantly for one can be disastrous when applied to others. Jonas Salk's polio vaccine, which contains dead virus, has been very successful. But using the same approach for measles only gives very short-lived immunity and in some children it led to an increased severity of the disease when the immunized eventually met the natural virus. We have been lucky with measles. Although it evolves in real time and lots of mutations have been identified in all of its six genes, these changes haven't affected immunity: live vaccine virus derived from a strain isolated in 1954 protects today as well as it ever did. And for most of us we have been lucky with syphilis. The *Treponema* has evolved to become a super-specialist, and whereas the bad news is that it hides so successfully from our immune response that no vaccine is likely ever to be developed, the good news is that even though we can't immunize against it, we can treat it extremely well because, not requiring the genes that it would need to live free in the environment, it has lost them (it only has 1,125 genes in total, whereas *E. coli* has four times as many) – including the genetic ability to become penicillin resistant. Each microbe has its own rules. Evolution has seen to that – the topic of our next chapter.

THREE

The Advance of the Mutants, and Other Novelties

Only religious fundamentalists deny that microbes evolve. Bacteria do it in real time, and some viruses like HIV have such high mutation rates that their population in an infected person is made up of a cloud of mutants; they are quasi-species. This chapter looks at what microbes' evolution means for our battle against infection – the moving target which means that, for all our scientific advances, we are always racing to stay one step ahead. The chapter begins by consider newly evolved bacteria that cause food poisoning, *E. coli* clones and *Salmonella* enteritidis, and then considers another, *Campylobacter*, that has piggybacked on the massive increase of poultry meat consumption in the last half-century made possible by the application of genetics to chickens. For the diseases caused by these organisms, antibiotics are not recommended and for some they are harmful – in those instances, a post-antibiotic era would be unproblematic, and might even be a good thing. But as this chapter goes on to discuss, the threat of antibacterial resistance looms large, and is explored in relation to gonorrhoea and MRSA. Not all microbial novelties are brand new in evolutionary terms. Case studies at the end of the chapter show that viruses from bats, including rabies, SARS and Ebola, can be nastier than anything created by Bram Stoker.

E. coli

Theodore Escherich was a paediatrician in Munich when in 1885 he identified the bacterium now named after him, *Escherichia coli.*[24] He was investigating the bacteria in the intestines of new-born infants. It was clear that these bacteria came from the mother, and that they were harmless. They had just established themselves as part of the normal flora. They live in animal intestines too. The world population at any one time is about a hundred billion billion.

For nearly a century, *E. coli* was a name familiar only to clinicians, municipal engineers (as an indicator of faecal contamination of drinking water) and bacteriologists. Pioneer molecular biologists in the 1940s picked it as their model organism because at that time it was safe to play with in the laboratory. However, in 1947 it drew the attention of bacteriologists by causing an epidemic of gastroenteritis among babies in Aberdeen; 219 fell ill and 99 died.[25] *E. coli* strains had not been implicated in gastroenteritis before. More than half of the babies infected fell ill after being admitted to hospital because they had other health problems. Today an outbreak of this scale would be seen as a national disaster of scandalous proportions. But in 1947 the infant mortality rate – the number of deaths per 1,000 live births in the first year of life – was five times higher than it is today. Babies died, mothers were upset, but this was as it always had been, and the media were not interested.

By the 1990s, public attitudes had changed, and a new clone, *E. coli* O157, had emerged. It first showed itself to be quite nasty by causing bloody diarrhoea in a Californian woman in 1975. For the next seven years there were only a handful of cases, and an outbreak in Oregon in the spring of 1982, in which nearly all the 25 sufferers had bloody diarrhoea and had eaten beef burgers not long before they fell ill, was thought to be an unusual one-off. But another burger-associated outbreak occurred a few months later in Michigan. All 18 cases also had bloody diarrhoea and 17 had eaten at the premises of the same burger chain within the previous 10 days. Outbreaks continued. They still did not get big media attention. The enormous outbreak in 1993 in the western states of the US was the turning point. Hamburgers from another chain were identified as the source: 732 fell ill, 195 were hospitalized, 55 developed the haemolytic uraemic syndrome and 4 died. The median age of the victims was 8.

It is the haemolytic uraemic syndrome (HUS) that makes *E. coli* O157 so dangerous. The bacteria do not invade the body – they stay in the intestines, but produce Shiga toxins (Stx). The Stx stick loosely to white cells in the blood and get transported to targets in organs with a rich blood supply. They cause harm by turning off cell protein synthesis. In the kidneys, which suffer most commonly in HUS, Stx also induce cells to commit suicide. Some patients with HUS die, not usually from kidney failure, which can be managed by dialysis, or even by a kidney transplant, but from brain damage or from heart dysfunction. The big problem is that once an infection with *E. coli* O157 has started, HUS cannot be prevented or modified by any therapeutic procedure. All that can be done with a middle-aged patient, for example, is to tell them prognostically that their chance of developing it is much less than if they were elderly or under the age of 10 (about 15% of these young people go on to develop it). But that is little comfort to someone bleeding from the backside and suffering severe abdominal pain.

In essence, *E. coli* O157 is a manure-to-mouth problem. Eating contaminated food has caused many dramatic outbreaks, but is far from being the only important transmission route. In August and September 2009, there was a very big outbreak affecting visitors to Godstone Farm in Surrey, situated just south of the M25 ring road round London.[26] The farm was used exclusively as a visitor attraction. Of the 93 infections linked to the outbreak, 65 cases were infected at the farm, not by food, but mainly during a visit to an animal barn, where some visitors petted sheep. Most cases were in children under 10 years of age. Of the 78 cases, 27 were hospitalized and 17 had HUS. Eight children needed kidney dialysis. The children with HUS had dialysis at the Evelina Children's Hospital in London. Its resources were stretched to the maximum. But two years later in Germany things were much worse – *E. coli* had demonstrated evolution in real time again, and had got even nastier.

The German outbreak was caused by a new organism, *E. coli* O104:H4.[27] This is a hybrid. It has an *E. coli* O157 Stx gene but its chromosome is mostly derived from another *E. coli*, called enteroaggregative because of the way it interacts with cells in culture. Fenugreek seed sprouts were the vector. Grown in Egypt, they left by sea in November 2009 in a sealed container, which was disembarked at Antwerp and then travelled by barge to Rotterdam and onwards by road to Germany.[28] In February 2010, 75 kg of the fenugreek seeds was delivered to an organic farm in Lower Saxony. The seeds were sprouted in late spring 2011, and were used as a garnish on salads. None of the victims could remember eating them, but the preponderance of women victims (68%) pointed to salads as a food type to investigate with vigour. At the beginning, the epidemiologists struggled. *E. coli* bacteria capable of causing gastroenteritis were found on Spanish cucumbers. The Hamburg Health Minister went public and the Spanish cucumber industry went into meltdown. But a detailed restaurant study comparing cases and controls who were not infected looking at receipts, menu, dish ingredients and photographs taken by groups in restaurants that happened to show food on plates exonerated the cucumbers and pointed to the fenugreek. The outbreak started slowly in early May but soon became enormous. Hamburg was its epicentre. At its end there had been 4,075 cases and 50 victims had died. The biggest difference between *E. coli* O157 and O104 was the much greater virulence of the new strain: 908 (22%) of cases developed HUS. Adults were not spared. The median age of HUS victims was 42. A particular feature of the HUS was that in many the brain was affected, with

20% of patients having epileptic fits. Fortunately, most of them seem to have made a good neurological recovery.

Whether *E. coli* O104 continues to lurk in Egypt is uncertain. The authorities there have vigorously denied that it was the source, but the circumstantial evidence is very strong. Given the political situation in that country, it is reasonable to guess that uncertainty is likely to continue for a long time.

Salmonella

Salmonella is another bacterium which is an ever-present danger owing to its ability to evolve new strains in short timeframes. Bacteriologists classify all *Salmonella* bacteria as belonging to the same species, *enterica*, but the name covers hundreds of different clones. Some, like *Salmonella* typhi, the cause of typhoid, only infect one species. But many are much less fastidious. The most versatile is *Salmonella* Enteritidis. Ever since bacteriologists started looking for it in cases of food poisoning, it has never been rare. But it took off in 1983.[29] In 1981, there were 1,087 cases recorded in England and Wales, and there were 1,101 in 1982. In 1983, the case count rose to 1,774, and it then increased steadily, reaching a peak of 23,231 in 1997. Similar rises happened in

Europe and in the US, where in the latter case the infection rate rose from 0.55 per 100,000 in 1976 to a peak of 3.9 per 100,000 in 1995. There had been a pandemic – the organism had taken off world-wide.

Eggs were the big problem. *Salmonella* Enteritidis had evolved to become an aggressive invader of the reproductive tract of the chicken, the bacteria settling inside the eggs. But the relationship between the *Salmonella* and the chicken was subtle, in that the birds remained well and were still good layers although infected. When this evolutionary step took place, we do not know. *Salmonella* Enteritidis control measures using better hen house hygiene and chicken vaccination have been quite successful. By 2012, the number of human cases in England and Wales had fallen from the outbreak peak in 1997 by more than 90%. *Salmonella* food poisoning has not gone away, however, with 8,003 cases diagnosed in 2012, some 30% of which were contracted during foreign travel.

Mutant chickens and Campylobacter

In general, eating poultry is a good thing. The massive increase in consumption after World War II and its big boost to protein in our diet had a lot to do with transforming tuberculosis from a killer disease to a silent infection with no clinical consequences (as seen in chapter 2). In 1948, 1 million chickens were consumed in the UK; in 2008, the number had risen to 125 million. Providing this vast amount of meat affordably has been made possible by breeding; in strict genetic terms, it has been due to the advance of the mutant chicken. Broilers account for most consumption. They have a high conversion rate of feed to meat, grow quickly and have big breast muscles. Their production is highly controlled genetically. Three international companies do the breeding; 90% of world broiler production is in their hands. They select the most appropriate birds from their pedigree stocks to become the parents of the next generation. Pure lines are crossed to produce the final broiler parent stock, which is a crossbreed. Developing a new broiler takes about 10 years.

Against this background of our deliberate engineering of broiler chicken genetics, *Campylobacter* has piggybacked on the poultry boom thanks to its own genetic variability and evolution. It didn't figure as a cause of infectious intestinal disease in the textbooks until 1977, when a pioneer paper by Martin Skirrow[30] showed that it was a very common cause of gastroenteritis, and that being infected with it was linked to eating poultry dishes. It had gone unnoticed because bacteriologists were not using the right methods to grow it in the laboratory on account of it being microaerophilic (it doesn't like oxygen but thrives on carbon dioxide) and thermophilic (it grows better at $41.5°$ than $37°$), and because it rarely causes outbreaks (to return to a theme we picked up on in chapter 1). It took some time to start gathering data across the UK, but by 1981 *Campylobacter* had overtaken *Salmonella* in England and Wales with 12,168 laboratory-confirmed cases. In 2012, there were 8,003 reported *Salmonella* isolations, but 65,032 of *Campylobacter*. However, as an indicator of importance, even this big number falls far short of the real total. Many people suffer in silence and don't consult their general practitioner, and many of those who do don't have a stool test. A reasonable estimate is that 280,000 people are infected every year in the UK, and 1.3 million in the US. Most cases recover without specific treatment, but a small number recover from the acute illness but then develop Guillain–Barré syndrome, in which the nerves controlling the muscles come under immune attack, leading to paralysis.

Campylobacter was the biggest food-borne disease challenge facing the UK Food Standards Agency when it was established in 2000. It still is. About 70% of poultry carcases in shops are contaminated. Attempts to reduce this by keeping the bacterium out of hen houses using stringent hygiene measures have failed. In any case, it is at least as common as a contaminant on free-range birds as on those kept inside. It is good at causing disease because only a small number of bacteria have to be eaten to start an infection. Any hope of eradication is impossible because it is very common in wild birds, and the prospect of a vaccine is remote because of its genetic variability. Even working out its natural history still frustrates: the incidence of human cases in the UK rises sharply in weeks 21 to 24 (May and June); we do not know why. Neither can we be certain beyond reasonable doubt how many human cases have a poultry origin. The lack of outbreaks is the big obstacle, because comparing the food histories of groups of people infected at the same time by the same organism is a very powerful way of pinpointing the vector of their infections. Good evidence supporting the importance of chicken meat as a source of *Campylobacter* came from Belgium in 1999, however.[31] At the end of January, a fat-rendering company started to use transformer oil with high levels of polychlorinated biphenyls (PCBs) and dioxins to manufacture animal foods. They were found out in May, and at the end of the month the government ordered that all Belgian poultry and eggs be withdrawn from sale. On 2 June the European Community went further and ordered the destruction of all foods containing chicken produced by contaminated farms between 15 January and 1 June. Belgian poultry meat accounted for about 60% of sales. It disappeared from shop shelves for four weeks and the number of recorded *Campylobacter* cases fell by 40%. They rose to normal when the ban was lifted.

Antibiotic resistance

E. coli, *Salmonella* and *Campylobacter* prove to be tricky adversaries because of their ability to evolve mutants in short timeframes. However, where bacterial evolution is at its most menacing is in microbes' ability to develop antibiotic-resistant strains. Influential advocates have raised public awareness about antibiotic resistance to unprecedented levels. As a long-term broad issue, the 2015 UK Government National Risk Register of Civil Emergencies ranks antibiotic resistance with organized crime and climate change.

None of these are new problems. For example, Arrhenius wrote his classic paper on atmospheric CO_2 and the greenhouse effect in 1896. It was only just over a decade later that Ehrlich's success with salvarsan against syphilis stimulated a search for other antibacterial drugs.

The next one out of his stable, in 1911, tackled pneumonia. The commonest cause of pneumonia then (and now) is *Streptococcus pneumoniae*, the pneumococcus. Ehrlich developed a quinine derivative, ethyl hydrocupreine hydrochloride, commonly called optochin, which killed pneumococcus in the test tube and was very effective in mice. But it failed in humans; the pneumococcus developed resistance to it during treatment. Optochin was abandoned, however, not because of resistance but because of its toxicity – it damaged the optic nerve and sometimes caused blindness. The observation that bacteria developed resistance was forgotten.

It was a few decades later before antibiotic resistance garnered serious attention again. The Public Health Laboratory Service in England and Wales (now Public Health England) became part of the NHS in 1948, and an account of its history[32] describes the good news for the decade 1946–56 – 'the end of smallpox as a regular entry in the public health statistics, the decline in diphtheria from 12,000 cases a year to fewer than 100' – and the bad news – 'the greatest ever epidemic of poliomyelitis' – but finishes: 'though nowhere appearing in the national statistics, the decade saw the epidemic of infections due to antibiotic-resistant bacteria in hospitals'. The big problem reported here was *Staphylococcus aureus*, which Mary Barber had shown to be a hospital problem.[33] Between April and November 1946, 12.5% of *Staphylococcus aureus* strains isolated at the Hammersmith Hospital, where she worked, were penicillin resistant. Between February and June 1947, 38% were resistant. This was due not to resistance developing while patients were being treated, but to the spread of a penicillin-resistant strain in the hospital. Not only had some patients with infections caused by resistant strains never been treated with penicillin, but all patients with these infections had been infected by a single strain with the same fingerprint. In 1960, the year that methicillin came into use, Barber wrote,[34] 'Whatever the mode or origin of antibiotic-resistant staphylococci, their increasing incidence in hospital communities is undoubtedly due to a process of selection of such strains by the widespread and haphazard use of antibiotics, and their spread from patient to patient by cross-infection,' and 'the control of antibiotic-resistant staphylococcal infection is an urgent problem and is not simple. It requires the active co-operation of doctors, nurses, physiotherapists, porters and domestics. Scrupulous asepsis and barrier-nursing mean extra work for all concerned.'

Barber's obituary described her as 'formidable'. Very left wing, she was also a churchwarden and committed Anglican. She died in a car crash on the way to a CND meeting in 1965. Her evangelical zeal and strong personality led to substantial reductions in the frequency of staphylococcal antibiotic resistance in the hospitals where she worked. But preventative fervour among bacteriologists seemed to fade after her death.

Staphylococci developed penicillin resistance by producing penicillinase, an enzyme that destroyed the antibiotic. Methicillin was developed in response by the Beecham Research Laboratories in Surrey by chemically modifying naturally produced penicillin. They called it BRL 1241, and wrote in the *Lancet* in 1960:[35] 'Resistance to BRL 1241 comparable to that which exists to penicillin G would require the ability to inactivate BRL by a new penicillinase. Since cultures have not been encountered showing this property, it seems unlikely that the selection and proliferation of resistant strains will take place rapidly, if at all.' But methicillin-resistant *Staphylococcus aureus* (MRSA) strains were first isolated only a year later, and the first outbreak occurred in 1963 at Queen Mary's Hospital for Children at Carshalton, also in Surrey. MRSA spread to 8 of 48 wards, infecting 37 patients and killing one. In the late 1960s and 1970s, MRSA started to grow less common. We do not know why. At the time it seemed that worries were over. But new strains appeared in the 1980s, and in April 1992 an epidemic strain, EMRSA 16, appeared in Kettering, in Northamptonshire, infecting 400 patients and 27 staff in three hospitals. It spread quickly, first to 15 hospitals and 845 patients in neighbouring counties. By September 1994, it had spread by patient transfers and staff movements to 21 London hospitals and four elsewhere. By 2000, it was in hospitals throughout the UK.

MRSA strains have evolved independently on several different occasions across the world.[36] They have arisen from successful methicillin-susceptible strains – successful in that they were common in hospitals because they were already well adapted to transmission there. Mary Barber was right. By adapting the general principles she worked out in the 1940s, 60 years later we forced the retreat of resistant mutants of the commonest cause of surgical wound infections, *Staphylococcus aureus*; search and destroy policies against MRSA reduced the number of infections by over 80% in England between 2007/8 and 2013/14.[37] The same has happened in the US: invasive MRSA cases fell by 54% between 2005 and 2011.

Mary Barber was a practical person. She was much less concerned with the mechanisms used by staphylococci or any other bacteria to become antibiotic resistant than its detection and prevention. Environmental and behavioural factors are key to combating microbial resistance – we must not allow microbes to take advantage of opportunities we give them to employ their ability to mutate and evolve. Indeed, Alexander Fleming had sounded the warning in his Nobel Lecture on 11 December 1945.[38] He said:

Penicillin is to all intents and purposes non-poisonous so there is no need to worry about giving an overdose and poisoning the patient. There may be a danger, though, in underdosage. It is not difficult to make microbes resistant to penicillin in the laboratory by exposing them to concentrations not sufficient to kill them, and the same thing has occasionally happened in the body. The time may come when penicillin can be bought by anyone in the shops. Then there is the danger that the ignorant man may easily underdose himself and by exposing his microbes to non-lethal quantities of the drug make them resistant. Here is a hypothetical illustration. Mr X has a sore throat. He buys some penicillin and gives himself, not enough to kill the streptococci but enough to educate them to resist penicillin. He then infects his wife. Mrs X gets pneumonia and is treated with penicillin. As the streptococci are now resistant to penicillin the treatment fails. Mrs X dies. Who is primarily responsible for Mrs X's death? Why Mr X whose negligent use of penicillin changed the nature of the microbe. *Moral.* If you use penicillin, use enough.

Attention was paid to Fleming's views. In the summer of 1947, a Penicillin Bill was introduced in the House of Commons by Aneurin Bevan. The government had consulted Fleming about it. It made penicillin obtainable only by prescription from a registered medical practitioner. This was a necessary control measure. But big problems remain. In an ideal world, all infections would be treated with antibiotics appropriate for the causative bacterium and its antibiotic sensitivity. But the world is not ideal. In all countries, most antibiotics are prescribed empirically on clinical grounds. Even in hospitals in rich countries, the cause of common conditions like pneumonia is often never established. In general practice it is the rule. And many countries have never had a Penicillin Bill, so antibiotics are freely available without any controls except price. That is why, for example, multi-drug-resistant strains of *Salmonella* typhi are common in Asia. And there is a good deal of truth to the pessimistic view summarizing our ignorance about bacterial infections, particularly the ESKAPE pathogens (*Enterococcus faecium, Staphylococcus aureus, Klebsiella pneumoniae, Acinetobacter baumanni, Pseudomonas aeruginosa, Enterobacter* species), which are particularly common as antibiotic-resistant pathogens in hospitals: 'For most bacterial infections, minimal lengths of treatment have never been defined.

The benefit of antimicrobial therapy over placebo for many common infections remains murky. The use of combinations of antibiotics is widespread, without conclusive evidence of benefit in most circumstances. There are far more questions than answers about the utility of basic infection-control measures.'[39]

Antibiotic resistance has always been there, in that many bacteria are intrinsically resistant to many antibiotics. *E. coli* infections have never succumbed to penicillin. But are we on the verge of entering a post-antibiotic era for the rest? The answer is microbe-dependent. For penicillin and syphilis, it is no. For gonorrhoea, it is quite possible, and could be just round the corner. Analysing the likelihood of a post-antibiotic era must also consider the antibiotics. We entered the post-sulphonamide era long ago. But the antibacterial chemical nitrofurantoin, first synthesized in 1944, has been successfully used to treat urinary tract infections for 60 years without resistance becoming a significant problem. Although it is easy to select resistant bacteria in the test tube, they are enfeebled and don't grow well enough to cause clinical problems or spread from patient to patient, and thus the antibiotic continues to be effective.

So the notion that an apocalyptic post-antibiotic era will encompass *all* bacterial infections is wrong. But antibiotic resistance is a big problem in Intensive Care Units. Hospitals are still homes for gram-negative antibiotic resistant organisms (distant relatives of *E. coli*) that are not particularly virulent except in people already sick with other conditions and in those with intravenous and other invasive devices. Patients undergoing immunosuppressive cancer treatment need all the antimicrobial support they can get. Health tourism is helping to spread antibiotic resistance genes from Asia to Europe, and sex tourism is doing the same for the gonococcus which causes gonorrhoea.

The severity of the issue is shown by the fact that on 18 September 2014, President Obama issued Executive Order number 13,676, directing Federal departments and agencies to implement his *National Strategy on Combating Antibiotic-Resistant Bacteria* and address the President's Council of Advisors on Science and Technology report *Combating Antibiotic Resistance*. At the same time in the UK, former Goldman Sachs Chief Economist Jim O'Neill began his chairmanship of a Commission on Antimicrobial Resistance, reporting to the government. His February 2015 report identified five specific steps for action: increasing early science funding to tackle the problem; making existing drugs go further; supporting the development and use of relevant diagnostics; investing in the people who will solve the problem; and modernizing global-scale surveillance. These are all excellent recommendations. The simplest one to implement is to give microbiologists more money. The others are more difficult; politicians and economists cannot deliver them. For example, the diagnosis of the cause of pneumonia falls far short of ideal because it is very difficult to sample the lungs without contamination, so antibiotic treatment often has to be best guess. No simple solution to this technical problem is in sight. And the surveillance of resistance to all microbes is patchy and incomplete in rich countries, while it is hopelessly poor in the countries where most of the resistance evolves. The prospect of significant improvement is remote.

O'Neill's first step focuses on finding new antimicrobials. Discovering potential candidates will be a lot easier than putting them on a prescription, even if discovery will be more difficult than in the past because all the easy targets have already been hit. It is certain that many novelties will fail because of toxicity – the fate of optochin in the early twentieth century.

Talk of 'falling back into the pre-antibiotic era' is rhetorically powerful. It is pronounced with the best of intentions. It has been suggested[40] that without antimicrobials the rate of post-operative infection after hip replacement surgery could be 40–50%, and that about

30% of those infected would die. However, it is always important to cut through rhetoric: this estimate was based on extrapolations from the results of amputations of gangrenous limbs done on diabetics at death's door. It was scaremongering. Infection rates like these are *pre-bacteriological*, not pre-antibiotic. Even in the Crimean War, Florence Nightingale went out of her way to get simple 'stump pillows' for soldiers who had survived amputations on the battlefield. US Army pre-antibiotic era statistics for World War I are very detailed: 4,178 soldiers had amputations because of bone injuries; only 187 (4.47%) died. A big study of hip replacements in 1981 showed that prophylactic antibiotics reduced infection rates from 3.3% to 0.9% in conventional operating theatres but showed no benefit in hypersterile theatres. Bacteriologically aware practices are incredibly effective (as Mary Barber made clear) and it is failures here which are responsible for causing such bad outcomes.

Bats and rabies, SARS and Ebola

Changed behaviour and practice, based in scientific knowledge, has succeeded in reducing the transmission of rabies to humans from infected dogs. However, in recent years in South America more human cases of rabies have been contracted from bats than from rabid dogs, again showing the novelties and adaptations that mean microbes present themselves as moving targets.

The common vampire bat feeds at night, preferring a moonless one when it isn't going to be noticed by its enemies. It keeps its blade-like teeth sharp by thegosis, the grinding of its upper incisors against its lower canines. The bite is almost painless, and cuts deep. Bleeding is kept going by anticoagulant-containing saliva which runs down a groove on the front of the bat's tongue into the wound. Studying rabies virus in bats in the Amazon jungle, where the problem is greatest, is difficult. However, it appears that the vampires and the virus may co-exist quite well, illustrating an important principle, that bats can harbour viruses harmless to them, but lethal for humans. This is a principle that is not restricted to vampires. It applies with full force to vegetarian bats as well,[41] and the Ebola virus can be traced back to these bats.[42] The chain of transmission from bats to human beings is often through another animal. Hendra virus in Australia goes from flying foxes (fruit bats) to horses and then occasionally to humans (57% mortality), and Nipah virus in Malaysia went from fruit bats to pigs to humans (40% mortality). SARS in China went from bats to masked palm civets to humans. It also spread from person to person: 21% of cases were in health care workers. The SARS epidemic lasted from November 2002 to the middle of 2003, with 8,096 cases and 774 deaths, a 9.6% mortality.

In the case of Ebola, intermediate hosts are probably primates like chimpanzees and gorillas. Ebola virus blasts the immune system, causing early dysfunction followed by overdrive that damages blood vessels and clotting mechanisms, resulting in bleeding and organ damage. There is massive cell death, heart failure and the blood pressure collapses. There are three main kinds of virus: *Zaire ebolavirus* has caused 13 outbreaks, *Sudan ebolavirus* 7, and *Bundigbuyo ebolavirus* 2. The first Ebola virus outbreaks occurred in 1976: *Sudan ebolavirus* caused 284 cases (53% mortality) in South Sudan, linked to a bat-infested cotton factory, and *Zaire ebolavirus* caused 318 cases (88% mortality) in Yambuku, 60 miles south of the Ebola River, in the Democratic Republic of the Congo. Until December 2013, 2,322 cases had been recorded, the biggest outbreak being in Uganda from October 2000 to January 2001 with 425 cases (53% mortality).

Ebola's nastiness hasn't changed in 40 years. The recent Guinea/Liberia/Sierra Leone West African outbreak is said to have started in Guinea, with 'Child

Zero', who died on 6 December 2013 and came from a family that hunted bats. The outbreak has been an international emergency: at the time of writing, there have been over 27,000 cases (suspected, probably and confirmed) in the three countries, of which over 15,000 have been laboratory-confirmed; the deaths stand at 11,264.[43] All previous Ebola outbreaks occurred in other African countries that were not wealthy. But the outbreaks ended very much faster in them than in West Africa in 2014/15. Why? Control measures worked. Experience from these countries showed that within two to three weeks of the introduction of controls, virus transmission was interrupted and case numbers started to fall. The crucial difference in the recent West African outbreak is that controls have not been effectively implemented,[44] and the spread of the virus has been helped by local customs, particularly traditional funeral practices – washing and kissing the dead. Humans have unwittingly helped the spread. However, it is more complicated than that. Ebola has features which also make human efforts at reducing its spread more difficult to implement. For example, screening the temperature of passengers at airports came into fashion with a SARS outbreak in 2013. It was worth it, because SARS cases develop a fever about five days before they become infectious, so isolating or quarantining them interrupts transmission. But Ebola cases do not become infectious until they are ill. So screening will fail to identify people who have been infected but are still in the incubation period, which can last for up to three weeks – a further challenge in our battle against the virus.

Brand-new nasty bugs have evolved and will go on doing so for all time coming. Old ones have been helped by our changing diet. Those who predicted a lifetime ago that antibiotic resistance would be a problem have been proved right.

At the start of my career, many of my advisers firmly believed that the Surgeon General's book would soon be snapped shut. The medical microbiologist was about to join the tuberculosis specialist as a species moving towards extinction. But evolution and the emergence of new diseases have kept medical microbiologists in business, helped by new opportunities for bacterial transmission being provided by the unintended consequences of changes in our own habits, bad and good. The next chapter looks at this assistance.

FOUR

How Our Actions Help Bacteria to Win Some Battles

Bacteria are brainless but can be brilliant at taking advantage of our jobs, military propensities and bad habits. Anthrax, as we will see, illustrates them all, as an occupational disease, as a bioweapon and as a cause of death in drug addicts. Legionnaires' disease is equally anthropogenic but is very different because its lifestyle-dependence is associated with good things: air-conditioning, brewing beer, taking showers, package holidays and hobby gardening. Controlling both bacteria needs an understanding of their natural history – the learning of lessons. After any disastrous outbreak, this is the cry. Maybe some lessons are learned, but they are regularly trumped by forgetfulness, as illustrated by the case of *E. coli* O157 and butchers, *Clostridium difficile* in hospitals and *Salmonella* in chocolate.

Anthrax

Anthrax is mainly a disease of cattle, goats, sheep and other herbivorous animals living in countries with warm climates. Animals are most often infected by their food. They die quickly. In the terminal illness, the bacteria multiply in the bloodstream and the carcass is stuffed with them. If it is buried unopened when the animal falls, the bacteria die. But if the carcass is cut open, the air stimulates the formation of tough heat-resistant spores that survive in the environment for many decades.

In the nineteenth and twentieth centuries, anthrax in Britain occurred in two very different forms. In most cases it was contracted from imported spores of the causative bacterium, *Bacillus anthracis*. The more common form of the disease was often called the malignant pustule. This is a skin infection which starts as a pimple on an exposed part of the body, usually on the head, the face, the neck or the forearm. It stays localized and swells up over the next few days. When fully developed, it is covered with a black leathery scab, hence the name of the disease: *anthrakos* is Greek for coal. The skin lesion is painless. If left alone, it healed spontaneously in about 90% of cases, with full recovery. 'Malignant pustule' was a bad name. In the great majority of cases, it was not malignant, and it did not contain pus, so it was not a pustule. But surgeons a century ago treated it like a big pustule – an abscess. They cut at it, or scraped out its contents with a surgical spoon, or tried to excise it. This interference encouraged the bacteria to get into the bloodstream. When they did, septicaemia followed and this was fatal for the patient.

The malignant pustule occurred in workers handling imported hides, hair, bristles, wool and bones, which were turned into gelatine and charcoal. Desert- and jungle-dried bones from Africa, India and Pakistan were the most dangerous, but also the most valuable because they did not need an expensive de-greasing process. They had come from animals that had died naturally – some from anthrax – and the remnants of commercial interest had been left after natural decomposition. Importantly, though, this had not diminished the infectivity of the anthrax spores, which readily infected workers after import.

The rarer kind of anthrax was inhalation anthrax, caused by breathing in the spores. It was first diagnosed in Britain in the late 1840s, not long after the woollen mills in Bradford started to import mohair, with Van mohair from the Lake Van region in Anatolia, turning out to be the most dangerous product. Some developed malaise, aching muscles, fever and a dry cough for a day or two, appeared to improve, but then suddenly developed severe breathing difficulties and shock and died within hours. In others, the illness was even more rapid. A contemporary account[45] said 'a man in previous good health may be at work in the morning and dead at night ... no pain ... very slight cough, no expectoration, quick breathing, great exhaustion, weak rapid pulse, mind clear, cold extremities, clammy perspiration, death in 15–20 hours.' Some dropped down dead without warning. The workers in Yorkshire called it 'woolsorters' disease' because they (correctly) perceived a connection between opening bales of wool and sorting their contents, on the one hand, and a fatal illness, on the other.

Anthrax was made a notifiable industrial disease in the UK in 1895, and Orders in Council made under the Anthrax Prevention Act of 1919 prevented the importation of some dangerous materials. A government disinfecting plant was also built in Liverpool that used a combination of heat and chemicals to disinfect in a process called Duckering, after one of its inventors, Elmhirst Duckering, a factory inspector. All this came about because, although most cases survived, from time to time anthrax killed those who came into contact with anthrax-carrying imported materials, such as butchers, slaughtermen, dock labourers, fellmongers, hair curlers, carpet makers, brush makers, zoo keepers, tanners, bone grinders and Dundonian gardeners, who in the 1950s used fertilizer made from bones rejected by charcoal makers. As a result, the number of deaths from anthrax notified as being contracted from an occupation fell 10-fold during the first 50 years of the twentieth century, helped by the introduction of penicillin, which reduced the mortality in malignant pustule cases, also by an order of magnitude.

Moving on to the role of the military in our relationship with anthrax, humans have actively sought to help anthrax spread and infect. In 1937, concerns were raised in Britain about the possible use of biological weapons, and intelligence reports indicated that the Germans were developing devices that used anthrax spores. British investigators started work in 1940 at the Chemical Defence Research Establishment at Porton, near Salisbury. Work went in two very different directions, the cheap and the expensive.[46] Operation Vegetarian was low cost. In late 1942 and early 1943, five million ground linseed meal cattle-cakes were charged with anthrax spores by a team of 15 women from a Bristol soap factory, working at Porton in a small building they called the 'Bun Factory'. Boxes were filled with 400 cakes. Each cake contained 500 million anthrax spores, a lethal dose for a cow, a sheep or a horse. The boxes were sealed with sticky tape and had a metal ring for operational opening at the point of discharge of the cakes from the flare-chutes of bombers over German pastures, where they would be found and eaten by animals. Trials with uncharged cakes showed that even when sparsely distributed, they were readily sought out and eaten by grazing animals. The aim of the operation was two-fold. The German population would be deprived of meat and milk, but, more importantly, the operation would demonstrate the principle of retaliation in kind. The cakes were never needed.

The aim of the expensive project was to develop the 'N' bomb, after the code-name for *Bacillus anthracis*. The 'N' device was planned to be a 500 lb cluster bomb containing 100 4 lb bomblets stuffed with anthrax spores. The bomblets and some bigger devices were tested at 'X-base', Gruinard, a 211 hectare island covered by peat bog half a mile off the mainland in the West Highlands of Scotland. Devices were detonated *in situ*, or exploded while hanging from a gantry, or fired from mortars, or, in one instance, dropped 7,000 feet from a Wellington bomber (unsuccessfully, because the bomb fell deep into the peat). Effectiveness was monitored by using sheep tethered in rows at various distances from the detonation sites. It was concluded that exposure 200 yards downwind would be lethal for humans, and that on a weight-for-weight basis anthrax was 100 to 1,000 times more potent than the chemical weapons known to the British at that time. Annual soil samplings on Gruinard were taken from 1946 until 1969. They showed that the number of live anthrax spores was only declining slowly. A big survey in 1979 only detected them in the detonation area and it was finally decontaminated in 1986. Vegetation was removed by herbicide treatment followed by burning, and the whole area was then drenched with 5% formaldehyde in seawater. A mine detector had found a big fragment of the bomb that had been dropped from the air, and formaldehyde was injected deep at this site. Test results six months later were all negative, and a flock of 40 sheep grazed on the island for five months and returned to the mainland in excellent health. Gruinard is now safe. I was interviewed for a TV programme made on the island on 15 April 2010. None of us got anthrax.

Anthrax remained of interest as a potential weapon, and not just among the military. Amerithrax[47] was the code name given by the FBI to its long investigation to find out who laced five letters with enormous numbers of very pure (not weaponized) anthrax spores in 2001, a few days after 9/11, and sent them to media organizations and US Senators. Letters were posted on 18

September and 9 October. The spores in them caused 11 cases of inhalation anthrax, with five deaths: a photo editor in Florida, two postal workers in Washington DC, a hospital supply worker in Manhattan and a 94-year-old woman in Oxford, Connecticut. The last two cases were probably infected from cross-contaminated mail. Eleven cases had cutaneous anthrax, six were in postal workers and three in media staff. About 32,000 people started antibiotic post-exposure prophylaxis. Some were vaccinated. In November, the Centers for Disease Control and Prevention (CDC) in Atlanta were visited for the first time in its history by a sitting President. It is reasonable to speculate that Amerithrax coloured George W. Bush's thinking about Weapons of Mass Destruction and his decision to launch Operation Iraqi Freedom the following March.

The molecular fingerprints of all the *Bacillus anthracis* strains isolated during this episode – from human cases, contaminated postal sorting offices, mail boxes, media premises and implicated envelopes – were very similar to each other and to spore batch type RMR-1029, prepared by Bruce E. Ivins, a scientist working at the US Army Medical Research Institute of Infectious Diseases. The circumstantial evidence against him eventually became strong. He committed suicide on 29 July 2008, and the investigation stopped.

Amerithrax was home-grown, from a strain that had been isolated in 1981 from a heifer in Texas. Anthrax in Britain, however, continued to be caused by imported spores. Until 2009, sporadic cases of cutaneous disease occurred from time to time, associated with wool, bones, leather and animal skins from countries where animal anthrax was common. Two fatal inhalation cases had been associated with hide drums. But in 2009, a new kind of anthrax began to occur.[48] The outbreak lasted from December 2009 until July 2010. Most cases occurred in the Glasgow conurbation in Scotland. There were clusters of cases in Dumfries and Dundee as well, and it had also caused five similar cases in England and two in Germany. In many cases it was still localized, like the malignant pustule, but went deeper into the tissues than in these traditional skin infections. Sometimes it resembled necrotizing fasciitis. Swelling was notable and was disproportionate for a wound infection. Some cases developed meningitis, and others died very rapidly, one of them before getting to hospital and five on the first day of admission. Molecular typing showed that they had all been infected with an anthrax strain new to the UK, most closely related to strains isolated from goats in Turkey. All were heroin users. It is thought that 80% of heroin in the UK travels through Turkey from Pakistan and Afghanistan. Once again, humans had offered a new route for anthrax to infect people in the UK. A detailed investigation concluded that the outbreak had been caused by a single batch of heroin that had been contaminated in Turkey. It was possible that during its travels it had been contained in an animal skin. Heroin in Scotland is distributed through two networks, an eastern and a western one. In this outbreak, police investigations obtained reliable intelligence connecting supplies in West Central Scotland to dealers in Bradford with links to suppliers in the Netherlands, the Balkans and, crucially, Turkey, going back to a source in Afghanistan. The French called woolsorters' disease '*La maladie de Bradford*' – so the Yorkshire link persists. So far in the US, heroin users have escaped anthrax – the multi-ton batches of the drug trafficked there by sea from South America are not wrapped in hides.

Legionnaires' disease: A very modern condition

Microbes can cross our paths in many different and unexpected, everyday ways, as Legionnaires' disease demonstrates quite well. In 1973, a group of tourists returned to Glasgow from a package holiday in Benidorm. Many were ill. One died in the aeroplane on the journey home, a second died two days later and a third after a week in hospital. They had severe pneumonia. All the tests of the day were done. They failed to reveal a cause. The Spanish Franco government was pleased – it gave an honour to the Scottish virologist who led the investigation. Then in 1976 a similar kind of illness struck down 182 attendees at the Philadelphia State Convention of the American Legion. They had stayed at the Bellevue-Stratford hotel from 21 to 24 June. Thirty-nine other people who had been in the vicinity of the hotel also fell ill. Twenty-nine Legionnaires and five passers-by died. The mortality rate was 16%, nearly as bad as smallpox. The CDC at Atlanta investigated.[49] On the second day of testing, they ruled out Lassa fever. On the third day, typhoid and bubonic plague were eliminated. But no known microbial cause emerged, just as in Glasgow three years before. Then at the end of the year, earlier work was revisited. Spleens from guinea pigs that had fallen ill after being inoculated with material from dead Legionnaires were re-examined. It looked as though they might contain bacteria. Fertile hens' eggs were inoculated with the bacteria, which grew and killed them. *Legionella pneumophila* had been discovered. Blood samples from the Benidorm/Glasgow cases had been kept and could be tested. The same bacteria were the cause of their illnesses as well.

Legionella bacteria live in fresh water and moist soil. They are parasites of freshwater protozoa, particularly amoebae, and have special defence mechanisms to prevent their destruction once they are inside an amoebal cell. In their natural homes, *Legionella* are harmless for humans. But they can thrive in man-made aquatic environments like cooling towers, wet air-conditioning systems, whirlpool spas and shower-heads in hotels and hospitals. Their optimum growth temperature is 35°, so they need warm conditions. Aerosols are generated by these structures and fittings. Breathing in *Legionella* bacteria carried in the droplets is dangerous because the bacteria see human phagocytes – white cells whose normal function in organs like the lungs is to sweep up and destroy bacteria – as places to grow, just like amoebae, and infected phagocytes die. Smoking, chronic lung disease and having cancer or diabetes tip the balance in favour of a bad outcome.

The Glasgow tourists to Benidorm had put themselves at risk by taking showers first thing in the morning. The *Legionella* bacteria had built up in the water overnight. In Philadelphia, they were being blown out from the hotel air conditioning.

Legionnaires' disease has always attracted journalists. The CDC public affairs officer said that Philadelphia was newsworthy because of marching Legionnaires and coffins being lowered. And *Legionella* from the cooling tower at the BBC's own Broadcasting House in London in 1988 infected 18 of its own staff – in this big outbreak, there were 79 cases and three died. During the late 1980s in Australia and New Zealand, another *Legionella, longbeachae*, emerged. Its home is compost. It is now being found in Europe. There was a cluster of cases in Scotland in 2013. This came to light because of better testing, not because it is a new disease. A recommendation to wear a mask when potting or shovelling compost was controversial, and, again, proved an attraction for journalists.

Legionnaire's disease is entirely man made. Without factory cooling towers, brewing on an industrial scale, shower-heads in hospitals and hotels, water-based air-conditioning systems, ornamental whirlpools and potting sheds, it would be out there still waiting to be discovered.

Learning lessons

Supposedly, 'learning lessons' is a big benefit that comes from publishing reports of inquiries into outbreaks with attendant publicity. But however good we are at learning, we are even better at forgetting, and this is perhaps where we most help bacteria and other microbes in their onslaught. Chapter 3 described the enormous *E. coli* O157 outbreak in central Scotland in 1996. I conducted an inquiry on it for the UK government. The report was debated in Parliament. It got big publicity. It led to legislation that targeted bad butchers. Then in 2005 there was another big *E. coli* O157 outbreak, primarily affecting children attending schools in South Wales. The Welsh Assembly government asked me to chair a public inquiry.[50] It was easy to establish that the same food safety failings were causative in both outbreaks; the villain in South Wales was a bad butcher. My report concluded: 'I had hoped that the lessons from the shocking events in 1996 would stay in people's minds. But comparison of the failures that led to this outbreak in South Wales with those in the outbreak in Scotland shows that this has not been the case.'

The outbreaks of *C. difficile* at the Vale of Leven hospital (described in chapter 1) also led to a public inquiry. The outbreaks had marked similarities to ones that had occurred in England from 2003 to 2006. A detailed report on the outbreaks at Stoke Mandeville hospital was published in July 2006. Its recommendations were highly relevant to the situation at the Vale of Leven, but no attention was paid to them in Scotland. In his public inquiry report, Lord MacLean said 'lessons had not been learned'. So bacteria are good at exploiting human failings. It is no consolation that investigations into non-microbiological failures also disappoint. In 1990, in the final report of his inquiry into the Hillsborough Stadium disaster, Lord Justice Taylor said: 'It is a depressing and chastening fact that mine is the ninth official report covering crowd safety and control at football grounds.... That it was allowed to happen, despite all the accumulated wisdom of so many reports and guidelines, must indicate that the lessons of past disasters and the recommendations following them had not been taken sufficiently to heart.'[51]

Chocolatiers have had a similar problem. Many have ignored or been ignorant of the abundant evidence that their products and *Salmonella* have a relationship that is particularly profitable for the bacterium. It was a very costly oversight for Cadbury's. On 13 July 2007 it knew that it faced very bad publicity. Representatives of the company were awaiting sentence at Birmingham Crown Court. At an earlier magistrates' court hearing, they had already pleaded guilty to putting unsafe chocolate on sale, failing to alert authorities that *Salmonella* was in the chocolate, and seven other food hygiene breaches. The *Salmonella* had made more than 40 people ill, some of whom were hospitalized. On 16 July, Cadbury's was fined a total of £1 million and had to pay £152,000 in costs. The recall of its products had already cost the company £30 million, and the incident had led to a management reorganization and the loss of a senior executive.

The bacterium in the chocolate was *Salmonella* Montevideo, an uncommon *Salmonella* in the UK. Between March and June 2006, there was a significant increase in the number of infections. Fifty-three with the same antibiotic resistance profile had come to light in England and Wales. Five of the cases had contracted their infections abroad, and two had been infected by contact with another case. Of the remaining 46, 31 had an identical molecular fingerprint indicating a common origin, and an outbreak. Strains with this molecular profile were termed *Smvd07*. Three cases caused by this organism (one infant, one child and one adult) had been admitted to hospital. The geographical distribution of *Smvd07* cases suggested that the outbreak was caused by a nationally distributed food. Nine other *Salmonella* Montevideo isolates had been sent to the Health Protection Agency Centre for Infections Laboratory of Enteric Pathogens for identification between February and May 2006. It was known that they were from food but had been submitted without any other information. They were fingerprinted. All had the *Smvd07* profile. It turned out eventually that they had come from Cadbury's. By July, the number of outbreak cases had risen to 37. Food histories were obtained from 15 cases; 13 recalled eating Cadbury products, and another reported eating confectionery products but couldn't identify the brand. A 16th case in Wales also reported eating Cadbury products.

On 19 June, Cadbury's told the Food Standards Agency in London that *Salmonella* had been detected in crumb in January 2006. Crumb is the basic ingredient in chocolate products. It had gone into the seven Dairy Milk products and the 10p Freddo bars. The Food Standards Agency advised on 21 June that they should be recalled, which the company initiated two days later.

Cadbury's put chocolate on the market knowing it to be contaminated with *Salmonella*.[52] In the recall press notice, it said that it was present only in 'minute traces'. However, in an apology in May 2007 it had said: 'Mistakenly, we did not believe that there was a threat to health and thus any requirement to report the incident to the authorities.' Cadbury's was only found out because the *Salmonella* was an uncommon one. If it had been *Salmonella* Enteritidis, which at the time was infecting several thousand people every year, the 40 or so extra cases would have gone unnoticed.

The link between gastroenteritis outbreaks and the contamination of chocolate with rare kinds of *Salmonella* is well known. In Sweden in 1970 there were 110 cases caused by *Salmonella* Durham; there were 200 infections from Canadian chocolate balls in 1973–4 caused by *Salmonella* Eastbourne; Italian chocolate bars contaminated with *Salmonella* Napoli caused 272 cases in England and Wales in 1982; Belgian chocolate coins contaminated with *Salmonella* Nima caused an outbreak in Canada in 1985–6; and 439 cases in 2001–2 in Germany, Denmark, Austria, Belgium, the Netherlands, Sweden and the Czech Republic were caused by German chocolate contaminated with *Salmonella* Oranienburg.

Cadbury's didn't appear to have taken these incidents into consideration when doing its risk assessments; neither had it taken account of the findings of an investigation into another chocolate outbreak in Norway and Finland in 1987, in which 361 cases were caused by *Salmonella* Typhimurium. Contaminated chocolate from retail outlets contained only about 10 bacterial cells per 100 grams, indicating that eating fewer than 10 organisms was sufficient to cause disease. It is so low because the abundance of fat in it protects the bacteria as they pass through the stomach.

Cadbury's decided in 2003 to introduce an 'allowable tolerance' level for *Salmonella* in its chocolate. Rather than destroying a contaminated product, it would go on to the market if the numbers of bacteria in it were very small. It is a reasonable guess that an important factor influencing this decision was the long-held view that the infectious dose of *Salmonella* is high, perhaps as big as a million bacteria, a view that goes back to 'volunteer' studies done on small groups of healthy US jail prisoners in 1950 who were fed eggnog containing known amounts of *Salmonella* strains isolated from spray-dried whole egg powder. Cadbury's paid a heavy price for choosing to be ignorant regarding the well-known love of *Salmonella* for chocolate.

This example is only one of many that demonstrates our inability to act on lessons from the past. The British public has a touching faith in public inquiries. Usually they are chaired by judges. (The US Supreme Court takes a very different view and disapproves of judges being employed on non-judicial and politically controversial matters.) They are very costly because they involve lawyers. UK governments appreciate their value, but have been immunized against them by the Bloody Sunday Inquiry, which took 12 years and cost £191.5 million. It was the stimulus for the 2005 Inquiries Act. Eleven new inquiries have been established under it.

Most have dealt with single events; the biggest group has been those into outbreaks of bacterial infections (*E. coli* O157 in Wales, *C. difficile* in Northern Ireland and Scotland). Antibiotics are absolutely contra-indicated in *E. coli* O157 infections and prescribing the wrong ones is the major predisposing factor for *C. difficile* problems. Antimicrobial resistance wasn't the issue. Neither were the issues scientific. The three public inquiries spent more than £14 million to find out that fundamental problems were the failures to apply well-known preventive measures, like hand washing. The first big book describing the bacteriology behind preventive measures and their practical application was published in 1900[53] – its science has not changed since then. But the issue is always whether anyone is paying attention.

Public inquiries represent just the tip of the iceberg in the relationship between microbes and politicians – a relationship which is not always straightforward, as the next chapter shows.

FIVE

Politics

Since its introduction by the Republic of Venice in the fourteenth century to prevent the import of plague, quarantine has been a powerful manifestation of the intimate relationship between infection and politics, local, national and international. Three-quarters of a millennium on, its principles are unchanged, and its enforcement is still demanded by the public (as shown by the case of Kaci Hickox in chapter 1). Pandemics are particularly political at all levels; case studies here of influenza and cholera illustrate historical and contemporary problems. HIV politics are well known, but the focus here is on a less familiar aspect: the politics of its science, the Nobel Prize and American exceptionalism. Foot and mouth disease does not infect humans but has caused enormous collateral damage to them. It is even more political than HIV, justifying it as a case study of British exceptionalism. The chapter concludes by considering eradication endgames.

Influenza: The slippery disease

Predicting influenza pandemics and their impact is a fool's game. It falls into the category defined by the nuclear scientist Alvin Weinberg as 'trans-science': questions that can be stated in the language of science but cannot be answered by it.[54] That is not to say that our inability to predict the timing of the next pandemic or its effects mean that planning is a waste of time. That would be like a householder saying because it is impossible to predict when they will be burgled or flooded that taking out insurance is unnecessary. But the only certain thing about influenza is that most of our predictions will be wrong. It is proved by the past; our influenza track record has been very lacking in foresight.

While statisticians have been studying its coming and going continually since the 1840s, we are still very uncertain as to how its eight genes interact to make one flu virus more virulent than another. And for prediction, uncertainty is massively amplified by evolution – frequent and random genetic mutations and the swapping of genes between bird, pig and human viruses.

The starting point for all influenza planning is the 1918 pandemic. It occurred in three waves. The deadly ones were in October 1918 and February 1919, when 20% developed lung complications of which 8% were fatal. It was thought that the pandemic was caused by a swine virus. Millions of people died across the world, more than all those who perished in World War I; it killed more US soldiers than the Germans.

David Lewis was an 18-year-old US Army recruit at Fort Dix, New Jersey. On 4 February 1976 he developed a respiratory infection. Against medical advice he went on a forced five-mile march. He collapsed and died that night. Influenza H1N1 of the swine subtype was isolated post-mortem. Other recruits also had flu. Eight flu viruses were isolated from them. Four were the usual seasonal one, but three were swine. Many meetings were held at the CDC in Atlanta. The consensus view was that pandemics happened about every 10 years; the last pandemic (Hong Kong, H2N2) had happened in 1968, so time was ripe for another. A memorandum went to the President in mid-March. The possibility was floated that the virus could kill one million Americans in 1976. On 24 March, a 'Blue Ribbon Panel' of experts met with President Ford in the Oval Office. A vaccination programme for the whole population costing $135 million was authorized, starting in October. There was a suggestion that a possible complication might be Guillain–Barré syndrome, which, as we noted in chapter 3, is a form of muscle paralysis. A few cases in the tens of millions of those vaccinated were diagnosed, and the programme was suspended, never to restart, on 16 December. Swine flu never spread and there was no pandemic. Heads rolled, including that of the Director of the CDC, and there was an inquiry.[55] We now know, moreover, that the 1918 pandemic virus did not come from swine but from birds, and that pandemics do not occur every 10 years.

Pandemic planners in the late 1990s and early 2000s still remembered 1918, but were driven much more by the bird flu H5N1. This virus came to attention in Hong Kong in 1997.[56] It killed chickens, but also infected humans. Sixteen fell ill and six died. The virus spread to other countries in the Far East, and to Egypt. The UK Pandemic Plan made the assumption that the next pandemic would be caused by a bird virus; that it was most likely to emerge in China or the Far East; that it would build momentum there before spreading to the UK, with estimates of the mortality rate being available before its arrival; that once it came it would spread to all major UK centres of population within one to two weeks; and that it would probably be a hot virus that would cause between 55,000 and 750,000 deaths. But when it came in 2009 the virus had not read the plan.[57]

It came from swine. It originated in Mexico. Only four days elapsed before its identification there and its arrival in the UK. It did not spread rapidly to all population centres; it affected the West Midlands and the Clyde Valley earlier than other areas. And the number of deaths by the end of the second and last wave was far lower than the most pessimistic predictions: the virus killed 457.[58]

The world was lucky. But pandemic planners still have to take into account the persistence of H5N1, which is fatal in a high proportion of cases. It has not gone away. Neither has another cause of pandemics, cholera, even though it is far easier to treat and prevent than influenza.

Cholera

Cholera can kill faster than any other infection. It is severe in up to 20% of those it infects. Painless diarrhoea starts without warning. Victims purge one litre per hour of fishy-smelling stools that look like ricewater. Severe dehydration develops very fast. Blood pressure drops like a stone, and the eyes become very sunken. They are dry because tear production stops. The hands and feet become wrinkled – classically known as 'washerwoman's fingers'. Shock develops. The blood becomes acid, and breathing becomes deep, laboured and gasping. Within hours, the victim dies.

The natural home of the causative organism, *Vibrio cholerae*, is the Indian subcontinent. From time to time it travels to other continents to cause pandemics. The first started in 1817 and spread as far as Nagasaki in Japan and Astrakhan in South-East Russia. The second started in 1826 and had spread to Europe by 1831. We are currently experiencing the seventh.

All these properties oblige politicians to take an interest in cholera. Today we praise the work of nineteenth-century English physician John Snow, in particular his demonstration of the link between an outbreak of cholera in central London in August and September 1854 and the drinking of water from the Broad Street pump. There were 616 deaths, nearly all of the victims living within a short distance of the pump. There was a brewery just round the corner. It employed more than 70 workers, none of whom died. The brewer allowed them free beer and did not think that they drank water at all. There was no cholera in Hampstead, but a widow there liked the water from the Broad Street pump so much that she had a bottle of it brought regularly by cart. She died of cholera. Snow saw the Board of Guardians of the parish on the evening of 7 September. His account says: 'In consequence of what I said, the handle of the pump was removed on the following day.'[59]

The pump handle has become a public health icon. It is commonly perceived that its removal stopped the outbreak. But it did not. Why the outbreak stopped, we will never know. In his own account, Snow says that 'the attacks had so far diminished before the use of the water was stopped, that it is impossible to decide whether the well still contained the cholera poison in an active state, or, whether, from some cause, the water had become free from it.' And his table of fatal cases shows that 516 fell ill before the removal of the handle, and that the outbreak had peaked on 1 and 2 September with 143 and 116 cases, respectively. By 7 September, the number of cases was declining fast. Only 28 fell ill on that day.

Snow's researches were masterly. In the light of all that has been discovered since, he got everything right. But the general acceptance of water as the main transmission route did not happen until almost forty years later. Hamburg was the turning point.[60] In August 1892, North Germany was experiencing a heat wave. The water level in the River Elbe was low and the tide pushed further upstream than usual. Two cases of cholera were reported on 16 August. Two died from it the following day. Case numbers then shot up, reaching a peak at the end of the month with more than 900 cases every day on 26, 27, 28, 29 and 30 August. The outbreak continued well into October. At its end, there had been 16,956 cases and 8,605 deaths. At that time, Hamburg was a city state in the German Empire. It had its own Senate and Citizens' Assembly. Altona was part of the Hamburg conurbation, but politically it was in Schleswig-Holstein. It was administered separately by Prussia. Altona had hardly any cholera in 1892. An apartment block, the 'Hamburger Hof', was on the boundary – it was in Hamburg but took water from Altona. None of its 345 inhabitants fell ill. Altona took its water from the Elbe downstream of Hamburg. It went through a sand filter bed. Hamburg water was taken from the river 2 kilometres upstream of the city and was not filtered. The link with transmission via water was clear.

Even now that water is known to be a transmission source, outbreaks can still happen, often as a result of deliberate political decisions. In mid-October 2010, the first cluster of cholera cases occurred in the village of Meille in Haiti.[61] The country had never experienced cholera before, and patterns of trade and travel to the country had protected it during all the nineteenth- and twentieth-century pandemics. In Meille, the first

patients fell ill on 14 October. Meille hosted a United
Nations Stabilization Mission (MINUSTAH) camp, set
up in the aftermath of the Port-au-Prince earthquake
on 12 January 2010, which measured 7.0 on the Richter
Scale and had killed 316,000 people. Nepalese soldiers
started to arrive at the camp on 9 October. Sewage from
the camp discharged from time to time into a stream
used by the villagers for drinking and cooking. The
stream flowed into the Artibonite River. An explosive
outbreak started in communities along the river. The
first indication that it had begun came from a village
where three children had died at school from acute
watery diarrhoea. The victims had drunk water from
the river and few had access to a latrine. People fled and
cholera spread. The epidemic in Port-au-Prince at its
beginning in late October was described as moderate,
with an average of 76 cases every day, but by mid-
December there had been 20,000. By June 2014 there
had been 703,510 cases and 8,552 deaths across the
country. Before the earthquake, only 63% of Haitians
had access to water from a pipe or a well, and only 17%
had access to a latrine. The safest place to be after the
earthquake was with hundreds of thousands of others
in an internally displaced person (IDP) camp, because
water safety and sanitation was better in them. Early in
the epidemic the mortality rate in the country as a

whole was 6.2%. Deaths occurred rapidly, with the median time from the beginning of symptoms to death being 12 hours in the community and 20 hours in hospital. By April 2011, the mortality rate had fallen to under 1%. A vigorous public information campaign was important. *'Jete poupou ak vomisman nan latrin'* (throw faeces and vomit into a water/earth closet) and *'lave men nou ak savon ak dlo pwop'* (wash hands with soap and clean water) were key messages. But by far the most important message was to prepare *'sewom oral'* – oral replacement therapy (ORT) – made either from a sachet or, as the Haitian creole information sheet says, *1 Gal dlo trete* (water with a chlorinating tablet added) with a demi teaspoon of *sel* (salt) and six of *sik* (sugar). The sugar with the salt creates an osmotic force that drives fluid back into the spaces between the intestinal cells, reversing the effect of the cholera toxin. In hospital, a cholera cot, a camp bed with a hole and a bucket, allows the diarrhoea to be measured and guides the ORT treatment. ORT is cheap and simple. It was introduced in the early 1970s and its use reduces the mortality rate of severe cholera 50-fold.

The geographical and epidemiological link with the Nepalese peacekeepers and the introduction of cholera into Haiti is very strong. There was a cholera outbreak in Nepal just before they left. But whole-genome sequence typing (WGST) put the strength of the link far beyond doubt. It fingerprints the bacteria to a higher resolution, and much more accurately, than fingerprinting does for fingers. The cholera bacteria that caused the outbreak in Nepal fell into four closely related groups. One of these groups had members that for all practical purposes were identical to the Haitian bacteria. All the Haitian cholera bacteria were identical, indicating that they were introduced to the country on a single occasion from a single source.

So far neither an apology or compensation has come from the UN. The issue is now with the lawyers. The UN claims immunity and the US government is acting on its behalf. The issue is now in the US courts. On 11 January 2015, Judge J. Paul Oetken of the US District Court in Manhattan dismissed a class action by Haitian victims on the grounds that the UN is immune from legal action unless it waives its immunity itself. An appeal is planned.

Sexually transmitted diseases: HIV

Sexually transmitted diseases (STDs) have always been political. When the Court of Baillies of Aberdeen met on 24 April 1497, it resolved for the eschewin of the infirmities comin out of France and strange parts that all light weman be chargit and ordanit to desist fra their vice and syne of venerie and all their buthes and houses [brothels] skalit [closed] and thai to pass to wark for thar sustentatione under the payne of ane brand of the yrne [iron] on ther cheks and bannysone [banishment] of the toune.

The 'infirmity' was syphilis. HIV has now replaced it as the nastiest STD. Everyone knows that it is a very political subject, involving people with strong personalities. It is not possible to do justice to the activities of individuals like Dr Manto Tsabalala-Maimang in South Africa and Randy Shilts in the US in a book of this size. The story of HIV science is also complicated with many colourful participants. A simple but revealing way to tell it is through the prism of the Nobel Prize. It demonstrates that science politics can be as vituperative and vicious as politics conducted by politicians – and both encourage and hinder our advances against microbes.

Virologists classify HIV as a retrovirus. In other words, the genes in the virus particle are coded in RNA. After infecting a cell, an enzyme in the virus particle, reverse transcriptase, converts them into DNA, which then gets them permanently spliced into host chromosomes. The public story of this virus family starts on 9

February 1911, when Peyton Rous, a scientist at the Rockefeller Institute of Medical Research, submitted a paper to the *Journal of Experimental Medicine*. It described the transmission of sarcomas (a malignant cancer) in chickens by bacteria-free filtrates made from the tumours. This was a revolutionary advance in understanding cancer. Rous's paper was masterly. It was crystal clear, comprehensive and flawless. It has stood the test of time, but it was not greeted with any enthusiasm when it appeared. After all, chickens were different from humans. One British cancer specialist said to Rous, 'But my dear fellow, don't you see, this can't be cancer because you know its cause.' Rous was nominated for a Nobel Prize for Physiology or Medicine in 1926, but his work was not considered to be good enough. In that year the prize was instead awarded to Johannes Fibiger, a Danish scientist. Fibiger had claimed that feeding mice with cockroaches infected with a worm called *Spiroptera* caused cancer. The Nobel committee at the time described the research as 'immortal'. It was not. Its results could not be repeated. Subsequently, the committee turned its face against giving awards for cancer research and Rous had to wait until 1966 before he was awarded the Prize. He was 87.

The cancer virus he discovered is called Rous sarcoma virus, RSV. In the late 1950s and the 1960s, Howard

Temin established that RSV turned tissue culture cells into cancer cells, and that although RSV had an RNA genome, this process, and the growth of the virus itself, involved DNA. In 1970, he discovered an enzyme in the virus particle, reverse transcriptase, which makes a DNA copy of the RNA genome. David Baltimore made the same discovery independently at the same time. Temin and Baltimore were awarded the Nobel Prize in 1975. Simultaneous scientific discoveries of this kind are quite common. Science is very competitive, but it is also very open. The standing of a scientist depends on the publication of results, so rivals are well informed about each other's progress, technical approaches and thinking. Another such simultaneous discovery was that by Heinz Fraenkel-Conrat in the US and Gerhard Schramm in Germany that RNA from the tobacco mosaic virus was infectious on its own. Fraenkel-Conrat and Schramm submitted their findings to scientific journals three weeks apart. Each was familiar with the other's work from the scientific literature, but did not know each other personally. This was not surprising. Fraenkel-Conrat was Jewish, trained in medicine in Breslau, but left Germany in 1933 for Scotland, Brazil and finally California. Schramm was a committed Nazi, a member of the NSDAP and the SS. In 1958, Rous, Schramm and

Fraenkel-Conrat all received the Albert Lasker Basic Medical Research Award.

Inspired by this discovery, the French scientist Luc Montagnier decided to become a virologist in 1957. Montagnier started a new virus research unit at the Institut Pasteur in 1972. Working with Françoise Barre-Sinoussi, in January 1983 he grew a retrovirus from a lymph node biopsy from the neck of a patient in the early stage of AIDS. It was human immunodeficiency virus – HIV. More isolates were made from other infected patients. A significant amount of research consolidating the link was also done in the US by Robert Gallo. Montagnier and Gallo both applied for AIDS blood test patents, leading to an international dispute. It appeared to be settled when France and the US agreed to share the royalties, and when President Ronald Reagan and Prime Minister Jacques Chirac gave a joint press conference in March 1987 saying that Montagnier and Gallo had independently identified the AIDS virus. But more information emerged, and the Nobel Committee gave the Prize to Montagnier and Barre-Sinoussi in 2008 'for their discovery of human immunodeficiency virus'.

Priority disputes are normal in science. Nationalism gives them strength. But they don't often involve heads of state. Nor do national legislatures weigh in that often on scientific research, but that is what happened to David Baltimore, the co-discoverer of reverse transcriptase. The saying 'academic politics are so vicious because the stakes are so low' has been attributed to Richard E. Neustadt, co-author of the report commissioned by the US government on policy making during the 1976 swine flu non-pandemic. The politics were vicious for David Baltimore, but the stakes were not.[62] After his Nobel, he stayed at the Massachusetts Institute of Technology (MIT) but moved the focus of his research from virology to immunology, and in 1990 he became President of the Rockefeller University in New York. At this time he was embroiled in a case of supposed scientific fraud committed by one of his collaborators involving a 1986 scientific paper of which he was a co-author. Congress became involved because of the enormous amounts of public money being spent on medical research. Laboratory records were examined by the Secret Service, hearings involved many lawyers, documents were deliberately leaked, and rivalry between scientists at MIT and Harvard fed the bitterness. Baltimore resigned from the Rockefeller in December 1991, after 18 months, because he said the issue had 'become a drag on my effectiveness'.

The fundamental rationale of HIV treatment today rests entirely on the discoveries made by Temin and

Baltimore: antiretroviral drugs block the action of reverse transcriptase and the virus enzyme that cuts HIV polyproteins. In Britain, Baltimore would have been offered a knighthood. Shall we call the troubles he experienced an example of American exceptionalism? Politics damaged Baltimore's scientific career. Only in that country would someone with his achievements have been so publicly humiliated. He is in good company. Exactly the same happened to the scientific director of the Manhattan Project that developed the atomic bomb, J. Robert Oppenheimer, also for trivial reasons enhanced by professional rivalry. However, there is British exceptionalism too, an excellent example of which is the way the UK has coped with foot and mouth disease.

Foot and mouth disease: A very political pathogen

Foot and mouth disease stopped being continually present – endemic – in Britain in 1889. Outbreaks caused by foreign viruses continued to occur, however, and big epidemics in Cheshire from 1922 to 1924 led to the adoption of the slaughtering of infected animals – stamping out – as the control measure. The aim was to emulate Australia (last outbreak 1870) and the US (last outbreak 1929), even if, unlike them, Britain was a meat importer on a big scale, particularly from Argentina, where foot and mouth disease was regarded as mild and unimportant. British veterinary inspectors were stationed in Buenos Aires from 1928 to try to ensure that when meat was exported, the disease disn't accompany it.[63]

The virus spreads more easily than any other. It travels on the wind. Virus from infected cattle in Brittany in 1981 blew across the English Channel and caused a small outbreak in the Isle of Wight. It was expected – meteorologists had accurately predicted its landfall – and cows are very susceptible: the threshold for infection is less than 0.1 virus particle/cubic metres of inspired air. Pigs are excellent spreaders because in 24 hours they breathe out 10,000 times more virus than a heifer, and sheep are particularly dangerous because they can excrete the virus during a silent infection when they appear to be perfectly healthy.

Unpredictability is another hallmark of foot and mouth disease. There were 179 outbreaks in the UK between 1954 and 1967. All were small, but the one that started in October 1967 expanded explosively.[64] It lasted 222 days and led to the slaughter of 434,000 cattle, pigs and sheep. Following a longstanding tradition, there was a government inquiry (there had been similar inquiries in 1922, 1924 and 1954), on this occasion under the chairmanship of the 10th Duke of Northumberland, an aristocrat, landowner and influential lay member of the scientific establishment. Then things went quiet. Better import controls aided by vaccination programmes in Europe and South America made things much safer. A government Contingency Plan was prepared in 1993 with working assumptions based on contemporaneous European experience. It was designed to deal with an outbreak of 10 cases. But on 20 February 2001, cases were diagnosed in pigs at an abattoir in Essex. The virus had been infecting animals since 7 February, and by the time the Essex diagnoses were made it had spread to at least 57 farms in 16 counties. Its dissemination had been speedy, because the first cases had been in pigs, the most efficient shedders of the virus; silent, because the pigs had infected sheep; and widespread, because the sheep were moving long distances to market.

Outbreak control was the responsibility of the Ministry of Agriculture, Fisheries and Food (MAFF). It struggled. There were big staff shortages. On 23 February, the government's Chief Veterinary Officer in England asked New Zealand, Australia, Canada, the US and the Republic of Ireland to help by sending veterinarians. On 27 February, rural footpaths were closed to the public. By 11 March, there were foci of infection from Scotland to Devon and in Wales. The Minister of Agriculture, Nick Brown, tried to reassure the public by saying on the BBC *Breakfast with Frost* TV programme that he was 'absolutely certain' that the disease was under control, but the number of cases went on increasing. Mathematical modellers and the government Chief Scientist met on 21 March. It was agreed that the outbreak was not under control. On 22 March, the government crisis response committee COBRA (after Cabinet Office Briefing Room A) was convened and Prime Minister Tony Blair took charge. He visited Cumbria, where many animals had been slaughtered but not burnt or buried. More than 40,000 carcasses lay rotting on the ground. The military had been called in, and Tony Blair asked the soldier in charge, Brigadier Birtwistle,[65] whether existing arrangements were sufficient. Birtwistle knew that an even bigger cull was imminent. He said no and Blair gave him *carte blanche*.

The outbreak peaked at the end of March and then wound down, slowly. The last confirmed case was in Appleby, Cumbria, on 30 September. A total of 6,456,000 animals were slaughtered: 1,291,000 from infected premises; 1,237,000 because of dangerous contact and because they were in contiguous premises;

1,510,000 because of dangerous contact in non-contiguous premises; 125,000 on suspicion; and 2,293,000 for welfare reasons, including lambs that had nowhere to go because of movement restrictions and an export ban. The outbreak cost the public purse £2.797 billion, of which £1.341 billion was paid to farmers. The tourist sector lost between £2.7 and £3.3 billion added value and industries supplying tourism suffered losses estimated at between £1.9 and £2.3 billion. Agriculture Minister Nick Brown was demoted while the outbreak was still in progress and left the government two years later. A heavy price was also paid by MAFF, which was dissolved and partially reinvented as the Department for Environment, Food and Rural Affairs, DEFRA. Closure of a kind was brought by the publication in 2002 of the report of an investigation by Dr Iain Anderson, the 'Lessons to be Learned Inquiry', the conventional and – as chapter 4 showed – questionably effective end to a politically mismanaged crisis.

Syphilis: American exceptionalism, again

In Britain, stamping out imported animal infections by a draconian slaughter policy has always been driven by political interests. It has its roots in the Cattle Plague

Act of 1866. In his 1867 classic essays on *The English Constitution*,[66] Walter Bagehot said: 'Parliament leans too much to the opinions of the landed interest. The Cattle Plague Act is a conspicuous instance of this defect. The details of that bill may be good or bad, and its policy wise or foolish. But the manner in which it was hurried through the House savoured of despotism.' The title of Bagehot's essays is misleading. They are as much about the US Presidential system of government as the British Parliamentary one. Bagehot wrote them soon after the end of the American Civil War. He says:

> The slave was formerly protected by his chains; he was an article of value; but now he belongs to himself, no one but himself has any interest in his life; and he is at the mercy of the 'mean whites', whose labour he depreciates, and who regard him with a loathing hatred. The greatest moral duty ever set before a government, and the most fearful political problem ever set before a government, are now set before the American.

It is reasonable to say that it is still a work in progress. Moral duty was certainly missing in the Tuskegee study on syphilis.[67] In 1932, the US Public Health Service set up a project in Macon County, Alabama, to follow black men who had had untreated syphilis for at least five years. 399 were recruited. The study was not secret. Many papers were published; the first, in 1936, was entitled 'Untreated Syphilis in the Male Negro: A Comparative Study of Treated and Untreated Cases', and the last, in 1973, 'Aortic Regurgitation in the Tuskegee Study of Untreated Syphilis'. When penicillin became the standard treatment for syphilis in the early 1950s, it was not given. A junior investigator in the Public Health Service expressed his concerns to the CDC in the late 1960s. But the study continued. In July 1972, he told an Associated Press reporter about it and the story ran in major newspapers. There was a public outcry. Senator Edward Kennedy held Senate Subcommittee hearings in February and March 1973, and treatment was authorized, stopping the study. President Bill Clinton and Vice President Al Gore made a formal apology at a White House ceremony on 16 May 1997.

Eradication endgames

Politics can be the last hurdle in disease eradication. Chapter 2 mentioned the drawn-out last stages of eradicating smallpox in Ethiopia and Somalia owing to civil war in the former and a war between the two countries. A disease currently in the throes of an eradication endgame is guinea worm disease – dracunculiasis – which is caused by a nematode, *Dracunculus medinensis*. Worm emergence often coincides with the planting and harvesting season and so as well as the human cost, the disease has important economic implications. The female grows to a length of 60 to 100 centimetres. It migrates from the abdominal cavity to the skin, usually on the leg below the knee, where it forms a very painful blister. The pain causes the sufferer to plunge the affected part into water. This stimulates the worm to release thousands of larvae into the water, where some are eaten by water fleas, *Cyclops*. The cycle of infection is completed when the next victim drinks the water and digests the *Cyclops*, releasing the larvae to burrow through the stomach and intestinal wall into the abdominal cavity. Interrupting transmission does not require high technology. Persuading victims to avoid seeking relief using a pond that is used as a source of drinking water, putting a parapet around wells, treating ponds with temephos, which kills *Cyclops*, and drinking water that has been filtered through a finely woven cloth all work well.

The global campaign against guinea worm disease began in the US at the CDC in 1980 and was adopted as a subgoal of the United Nations International Drinking Water Supply and Sanitation Decade (1981–90). The effort has been led since 1986 by the Carter Center, assisted by the CDC, the World Health Organization (WHO), the United Nations Children's Fund (UNICEF), the Bill and Melinda Gates Foundation, many other donors and the governments of the countries where the worm occurs. In 1986 the World Health Assembly of the WHO set 1995 as the target year for eradication. This target was not met, but there has been enormous progress. In 1986, 3.5 million people had guinea worm disease. In 2014, there were only 126 cases. We are in the endgame. How long the endgame will last is hard to say. There were 70 cases in South Sudan in 2014, a time of civil war, and 40 in Mali, where the eradication programme was interrupted for a time in 2012 by a military uprising. The big challenge to finishing off the worm for good is political. It is the same for polio. In 1988, the WHO set a target of eradication by 2000. Politics has interfered with its implementation. But the endgame is in play; in 2015 the only countries reporting indigenous paralytic polio cases are Pakistan and Afghanistan. As the number of cases diminishes to single figures, it becomes much more difficult to maintain the political will to prioritize eradication: '[S]ecurity, operational and political problems can suddenly arise ... the final stage of the march to polio eradication is a rocky road, as the polio virus fights to save itself from extinction.'[68]

This chapter has shown that politics and infection often have an uneasy relationship. President Jimmy Carter's Farewell Address on 14 January 1981 struck a bitter note:[69]

> Today, as people have become ever more doubtful of the ability of the government to deal with our problems, we are increasingly drawn to single-issue groups and special interest organizations to ensure that whatever happens our own personal views and our own private interests are protected. This is a disturbing factor in American political life. It tends to distance our purposes because the national interest is not always the sum of all our single or special interests.

Prophetic words decades later, in the light of groups refusing polio vaccine in the Muslim world and measles vaccine in Europe. It would be wrong to end on a negative note, however. Even though politicians prefer quick fixes, they still vote for funds to support basic research with practical applications that will probably not be realized – if at all – until long after they have left office, and the best continue to use their political influence thereafter. Indeed, in 1995, 14 years after leaving the White House, Jimmy Carter brokered the guinea worm cease-fire in Sudan.

To conclude, to return to the title question of this book, 'have bacteria won?', the answer is no. In countries as rich as the UK and the US, the graveyards are no longer full of tombstones memorializing our infants. The Black Death, diphtheria and continued fevers (typhoid and typhus) are history. We celebrate those who have discovered vaccines and antibiotics. But a central theme of this book has been the enormous importance of the unintended consequence. The chicken in every pot and the pasteurization of milk to extend shelf life turned tuberculosis into a shadow of its former self. Piping town water from reservoirs and lochs in the hills stopped cholera dead. The unintended quantitative benefits far outweigh the negative developments, even including such notorious examples as the feeding of young calves with meat and bone meal, which inadvertently spread BSE, and the introduction of cholera into Haiti by United Nations peacekeepers in 2010.

Alexander Fleming did not intend to discover antibiotics when in 1927 he started to investigate the pigmentation of colonies of *Staphylococcus aureus* growing on culture plates. In his definitive account of the discovery, Ronald Hare[70] (who, incidentally, gave me my first bacteriology job) said that it was 'the supreme example in all scientific history of the part that luck may play in the advancement of knowledge'. Essential factors in its discovery were: a cold summer; a fungus expert on the floor below who by chance had grown a powerful penicillin-producing mould whose spores had drifted upstairs; the very strong likelihood that when Fleming went on his summer holiday he had not put the famous Petri dish into an incubator; and a visit by a former assistant to whom he showed the already discarded dish, causing him to look at it again, and say, 'That's funny...'

Another big theme has been our propensity to forget the lessons and ignore the warnings from the past. Ignaz Semmelweis – an early pioneer of antiseptic practices – died in 1865, and Alexander Fleming warned about antibiotic resistance in 1945. But hand hygiene still often falls short, and those who buy, prescribe and regulate the use of antibiotics often seem to be unaware that bacteria evolve in real time, and that the use of any antimicrobial drug will lead sooner or later to the development of resistant mutants by natural selection.

New antimicrobials will be very welcome. Getting them ready for roll-out will be expensive and will take years. But past experience indicates that their abuse will start without delay. Preventing it in countries with poor regulatory systems will be much more difficult than making the discoveries. In all classes of therapeutic antimicrobials, resistance has developed, sooner or later. In essence, delaying it will be an anthropological rather than a scientific problem.

The big Ebola outbreak in West Africa in 2014/15 was no different, in the sense that interrupting virus transmission needed anthropologists, not scientists, to find out how to persuade people that funeral practices such as kissing corpses are dangerous. The same expertise is needed to work out how best to induce health care workers and cooks to wash their hands when nobody is watching, as well as to prevent HIV and other diseases transmitted by unsafe sex.

Cultural differences, such as traditional funeral practices, between West African countries and nations such as Uganda and the Democratic Republic of the Congo explain why outbreaks of Ebola ended much sooner in the latter. National differences have always been an important influence in determining antimicrobial tactics and strategies. North American countries dealt with diphtheria faster and measles more effectively than the UK because public health professionals and the public were more enthusiastic about vaccines.

Anne Schuchat was the lead public health doctor advising US citizens during the 2009 H1N1 influenza pandemic. Her appearances on TV and social media in a rear admiral's uniform gave her messages authoritative strength, as well as being a reminder of the military origins of the US Public Health Service and its offshoot, the CDC. The military metaphor was rubbished at the beginning of this book. But ever since the days of Florence Nightingale, war has played a very important role in the 'fight against the bacteria', even if Nightingale, when working at Scutari, was an enthusiastic miasmatist and firm believer in the spontaneous generation of germs.

During World War II, the US government set up the Office of Scientific Research and Development and the Committee on Medical Research. Established solely for military purposes, they chose the pharmaceutical companies responsible for the mass production of penicillin, and started many of the first clinical trials. The War Production Board funded production. It is certain that without these initiatives the introduction of penicillin would have been delayed for many years. They also helped to create today's massive pharmaceutical industry (Big Pharma).[71]

And in the UK, war gave a big boost to struggles against bacteria. Predictions in the 1930s that bombing would lead to epidemics and a fear that bacteriological weapons would be used led to the foundation of the Public Health Laboratory Service (PHLS) in England and Wales. The expected epidemics did not follow the Blitz, but the PHLS survived and grew. Sad to say, however, another myth, that of the closing of the books, has recently been working against it. The funding and independence of the service have come under attack and, thanks to political meddling and NHS 'reform', it is now a shadow of its former self. Even its US counterpart, the CDC, though lavishly funded in comparison, is trimming its aspirations. The Presidential Budget Request for financial year 2015 is for $6.6 billion, $243 million less than the allocation for 2014, even though it is asking for an additional $30 million to detect and prevent antibiotic resistance and $161 million for polio eradication.

The aim of this book has been to give an overview of our current relationship with microbes. Its biases come from my personal experience and British background. If I were German or French or American, they would be different, despite science being international and bacteria and viruses being beneficiaries of globalization long before Genghis Khan and Christopher

Columbus. Even so, national attitudes to microbes still differ a lot. It is the same for those deemed to have fought them successfully. In France there are 78 streets named after Louis Pasteur.[72] In Britain, the most abundant memorials to Joseph Lister, a contemporary of Pasteur who applied his ideas to develop antiseptic surgery, are the bottles of a brand of antiseptic mouthwash on supermarket shelves. The most secure memorial for a microbiologist is a different kind of eponymization. S. Burt Wolbach deservedly made it with *Wolbachia*. His studies on typhus in Poland in 1920 for the League of Red Cross Societies were definitive. He hatched typhus-free Canadian nits in a cage strapped to his leg, maintained the lice there in a journey from North America to Warsaw, and used them to confirm their role in transmission of a disease that was the Ebola of its day. His report is dedicated 'To the Memory of the Investigators of Typhus who as a Consequence of their Researches Contracted the Disease and Died: Conneff, Cornet, Jochmann, Lüthje, von Prowazek, Ricketts, Schüssler.' For them the bacteria had won.

It would be bad to end on a negative note. The CDC got influenza wrong in 1976, and syphilis wrong at Tuskegee, but its free peer-reviewed journal, *Emerging Infectious Diseases*, is a model of its kind. The cost of

DNA sequencing is decreasing and its power is increasing. Both are changing exponentially at rates outpacing Moore's Law, which 60 years ago rightly predicted that computer power would double every two years. This means that tracking microbes, understanding their evolution and finding their weaknesses gets easier, faster and cheaper every day. That is just as well since evolution has considerable power to surprise. It also places the onus on us with regard to how to manage our relationship with microbes and infectious disease.

To finally underline again that bacteria are not necessarily our 'enemy' – to 'question the question' that the title of this book poses – it is worth closing with the following example. While antibiotics and vaccines were great discoveries, the most important twentieth-century innovation in the 'fight against the bacteria' in terms of lives saved was the Haber–Bosch process,[73] the industrial synthesis of ammonia from hydrogen and atmospheric nitrogen. The synthetic nitrogen fertilizers it produces are essential for agriculture to affordably produce the levels of digestible nitrogen in our food that are needed to protect us from the bad effects of infection. Before Haber, apart from a trivial contribution from lightning, the only natural process that converted atmospheric nitrogen into a useful form was its fixation *by bacteria*, mostly ones living symbiotically in legumes such as clover. Unequivocally, they are good bacteria. Rather than fighting them, we have joined them, and indeed our chemical synthesis production now matches their outputs world-wide.

However medically inappropriate, the military metaphor is still used as vigorously as ever. But the microbes are losing. That the top enemy in the 'war' against death and disease is now cancer proves it.

1 Blake, D., Pickles, J. (2008) *Apocalyptic Demography? Putting Longevity Risk in Perspective*. Pensions Institute at Cass Business School, London (pp. 25–6).

2 Douglas, M., Wildavsky, A. (1983) *Risk and Culture*. University of California Press, Berkeley, London (p. 10).

3 Pennington, T.H. (2003) *When Food Kills*. Oxford University Press, Oxford.

4 The BSE Inquiry (2000) *The Report: Volume 1*. The Stationery Office, London.

5 Meleney, F.L. (1924) Hemolytic *Streptococcus* gangrene. *Archives of Surgery* 9: 317–64.

6 Pennington, T.H. (2010) The role of the media in public health crises: perspectives from the UK and Europe. In *Risk Communication and Public Health*, eds Bennet, P., Calman, K., Curtis, S., Fischbacher-Smith, D. Oxford University Press, Oxford.

7 Lardner, D.,ed. (1859) *The Museum of Science and Art: Volume 1*. Walton and Maberly, London (p. 181).

8 Pennington, T.H. (2004) Why can't doctors be more scientific? *London Review of Books* 26 (No. 13): 28–9.

9 State of Maine, District Court, Fort Kent. Docket No. CV-2014-36. *Mary C. Mayhew, Petitioner v. Kaci Hickox, Respondent. Order reference M.R.Civ.P.79(a)*. Charles C. LaVerdiere, Chief Judge, 31 October 2014.

10 Washer, P., Joffe, H. (2006) The hospital 'superbug': social representations of MRSA. *Social Science and Medicine* 63: 2141–52.

References

11 The Rt Hon. Lord MacLean (Chairman) (2014) *The Vale of Leven Hospital Inquiry Report*. APS Group Scotland.

12 Fenner, F., Henderson, D.A., Arita, I., Jezek, Z., Ladnyi, I.D. (1988) *Smallpox and Its Eradication*. World Health Organization, Geneva.

13 Moore, J.E. (1933) *The Modern Treatment of Syphilis*. Charles C. Thomas, Springfield and Baltimore (p. 39).

14 Mercier, C.A. (1914) *A Textbook of Insanity and Other Mental Diseases*, 2nd edition. George Allen and Unwin, London (p. 248).

15 Mott, F.W. (1910) *Syphilis of the Nervous System, Vol. 4*. In *A System of Syphilis*, eds Power, D.'A., Murphy, J.K. Oxford Medical Publications, Oxford (p. 275).

16 Hamlin, C. (2009) Cholera forcing: the myth of the good epidemic and the coming of good water. *American Journal of Public Health* 99: 1948–54.

17 Lond, R.E.C. (1903) quoted in Smout, T.C., *A Century of the Scottish People: 1830s*. Collins, London (p. 45).

18 Food Standards Agency (2014) FSA Board Decision on Raw Milk, *http://www.food.gov.uk/news-updates/news/2014/6130/rawmilk*.

19 Langer, A.J., Ayers, T., Grass, J., Lych, M., Angulo, F.J., Mahon, B.E. (2012) Nonpasteurized dairy products, disease outbreaks, and state laws: United States, 1993–2006. *Emerging Infectious Diseases* 18: 385–91.

20 Leyton, G.B. (1946) Effects of slow starvation. *Lancet* 2: 73–9.

21 Byrne, K, Nichols, R.A. (1999) *Culex pipiens* in London Underground tunnels: differentiation between surface and subterranean populations. *Heredity* 82: 7–15.

22 United States General Accounting Office (2000) *Report to Congressional Requesters. West Nile Virus Outbreak. Lessons for Public Health Preparedness*. GAO/HEHS-00-180.

23 Tamarozzi, F., Halliday, A., Gentil, K., Hoerauf, A., Pearlman, E., Taylor, M.J. (2011) Onchocerciasis: the role of

Wolbachia bacterial endosymbionts in parasite biology, disease pathogenesis, and treatment. *Clinical Microbiology Reviews* 24: 459–68.

24 Escherich, T. (1885) Die Darmbacterien des Neuegeboren und Sauglings. *Fortschritte der Medezin* 3: 515–22, 547–54.

25 Smith, J. (1955) *The Aetiology of Epidemic Infantile Gastro-enteritis*. The Royal College of Physicians, Edinburgh.

26 Independent Investigation Committee (2010) *Review of the Major Outbreak of E. coli O157 in Surrey, 2009: An Evaluation of the Outbreak and Its Management, with a Consideration of the Regulatory Framework and Control of Risks Relating to Open Farms*. https:// www.gov.uk/government/uploads/system/uploads/attachment_data/ file/342361/Review_of_major_outbreak_of_e_coli_o157_in_surrey _2009.pdf.

27 Frank, C., et al (2011) Epidemic profile of shiga-toxin – producing *Escherichia coli* O104:H4 outbreak in Germany. *New England Journal of Medicine* 365: 1771–80.

28 European Food Safety Authority (2011) Shiga toxin-producing *E. coli* (STEC) O104:H4 outbreaks in Europe: taking stock. *EFSA Journal* 9 (10): 2390–412.

29 Cogan, T.A, Humphrey, T.J. (2003) The rise and fall of *Salmonella* Enteritidis in the UK. *Journal of Applied Microbiology* 94: 114S–119S.

30 Skirrow, M.B. (1977) *Campylobacter* enteritis: a 'new' disease. *British Medical Journal* 2: 9–10.

31 Vellinga, A., Van Loock, F. (2002) The dioxin crisis as experiment to determine poultry-related *Campylobacter* enteritis. *Emerging Infectious Diseases* 8: 19–22.

32 Williams, R.E.O. (1985) *Microbiology for the Public Health*. Public Health Laboratory Service, London (p. 31).

33 Barber, M. (1947) Staphylococcal infection due to penicillin-resistant strains. *Lancet* 2: 863–5.

References

34 Barber, M. (1960) Source and control of antibiotic-resistant Staphylococcal infection in hospitals. In *Recent Advances in Clinical Pathology*, ed. Dyke, S.C. Churchill, London (p. 8).

35 Rolinson, G.N., Stevens, S., Batchelor, F.R., Cameron-Wood, J., Chain, E.B. (1960) Bacteriological studies on a new penicillin – BRL 1341. *Lancet* 2: 564–7.

36 Enright, M.C., Robinson, D.A., Randle, G., Feil, E.J., Grundmann, H., Spratt, B.G. (2002) The evolutionary history of methicillin-resistant *Staphylococcus aureus* (MRSA). *Proceedings of the National Academy of Sciences USA* 99: 7687–92.

37 Public Health England (2014) MRSA, MSSA and E. coli bacteraemia and C. difficile infection data: quarterly epidemiological commentary. *https://www.gov.uk/government/statistics/mrsa-mssa-and-e-coli-bacteraemia-and-c-difficile-infection-quarterly-epidemiological-commentary*.

38 Sir Alexander Fleming (1945) Nobel Lecture: Penicillin (p. 93). *http://www.nobelprize.org/nobel_prizes/medicine/laureates/1945/fleming-lecture.pdf*.

39 Rice, L.B. (2008) Federal funding for the study of antimicrobial resistance in nosocomial pathogens: no ESKAPE, *Journal of Infectious Diseases* 197: 1079–81 (p. 1079).

40 Smith, R., Coast, J. (2013) Antimicrobial resistance: the true cost. *British Medical Journal* 346: 20–2.

41 O'Shea, T.J., et al (2014) Bat flight and zoonotic viruses. *Emerging Infectious Diseases* 20: 741–5.

42 Pigott, D.M., et al (2014) Mapping the zoonotic niche of Ebola virus disease in Africa. *eLife* 2014: 3: e04395.

43 Centers for Disease Control and Prevention (2015) 2014 Ebola outbreak in West Africa – case counts. *http://www.cdc.gov/vhf/ebola/outbreaks/2014-west-africa/case-counts.html*.

44 WHO Ebola Response Team (2015) Ebola virus disease in West Africa – the first 9 months of the epidemic and

forward projections. *New England Journal of Medicine* 372: 180–9.

45 Bligh, M. (1960) *Dr Eurich of Bradford.* James Clarke, London.

46 Carter, G.B. (2000) *Chemical and Biological Defence at Porton Down 1916–2000.* The Stationery Office, London.

47 United States Department of Justice (2010) *Amerithrax Investigative Summary.* http://www.justice.gov/archive/amerithrax/docs/amx-investigative-summary.pdf.

48 Health Protection Scotland (2011) An outbreak of anthrax among drug users in Scotland, December 2009 to December 2010. http://www.documents.hps.scot.nhs.uk/giz/anthrax-outbreak/anthrax-outbreak-report-2011-12.pdf.

49 Etheridge, E.W. (1992) *Sentinel for Health: A History of the Centers for Disease Control.* University of California Press, Berkeley, and Oxford.

50 Pennington, T.H. (2009) *The Public Inquiry into the September 2005 Outbreak of E. coli O157 in South Wales.* http://www.ecoli inquirywales.org.

51 The Hillsborough Stadium Disaster, 15 April 1980. Inquiry by the Rt Hon. Lord Justice Taylor. Final Report (1990). HMSO, London (p. 4).

52 BBC News (2007) Cadbury's fined £1m over salmonella. 10 July. http://news.bbc.co.uk/1/hi/england/6900467.stm.

53 Haegler, C.S. (1900) *Handereinigung, Handedesinfektion und Handeschutz.* Benno Schwabe, Basel.

54 Weinberg, A.M. (1972) Science and trans-science. *Minerva* 10: 209–22.

55 Neustadt, R.E., Fineberg, H.V. (1983) *The Epidemic That Never Was: Policy-Making and the Swine Flu Affair.* Vintage Books, New York.

References

56 Pennington, T.H. (2005) If H5N1 evolves. *London Review of Books* 27 (No. 12): 39.

57 Hine, D. (2010) *The 2009 Influenza Pandemic: An independent review of the UK response to the 2009 influenza pandemic.* http:// www.gov.uk/government/uploads/system/uploads/attachment_data/ file/61252/the2009influenzapandemic-review.pdf.

58 Pebody, R.G., et al (2010) Pandemic influenza A (H1N1) 2009 and mortality in the United Kingdom: risk factors for death, April 2009 to March 2010. *Eurosurveillance* 15 (20). *http://www.eurosur veillance.org/ViewArticle.aspx?Articleid=19571.*

59 Snow, J., Richardson, B.W., Frost, W.H. (1936) *Snow on Cholera, being a Reprint of Two Papers by John Snow M.D. together with a Biographical Memoir by B.W. Richardson, M.D. and an Introduction by Wade Hampton Frost, M.D.* The Commonwealth Fund, New York (pp. 40, 51–2).

60 Evans, R.J. (1990) *Death in Hamburg. Society and Politics in the Cholera Years 1830–1910.* Penguin Books, Harmondsworth.

61 Piarroux, R., et al (2011) Understanding the cholera epidemic, Haiti. *Emerging Infectious Diseases* 17: 1161–8.

62 Kevles, D.J. (1998) *The Baltimore Case.* Norton, New York.

63 Woods, A. (2004) *A Manufactured Plague? The History of Foot and Mouth Disease in Britain.* Earthscan, London.

64 Anderson, I. (2002) *Foot and Mouth Disease 2001: Lessons to be Learned Inquiry.* The Stationery Office, London.

65 Birtwistle, A. (2001) Personal account. In *Foot and Mouth, Heart and Soul,* ed. Graham, C. Small Sister for BBC Radio Cumbria.

66 Bagehot, W. (1936 [1867]) *The English Constutution.* Oxford University Press, Oxford (pp. 144, 200).

67 Reverby, S.M., ed. (2000) *Tuskegee's Truths.* University of North Carolina Press, Chapel Hill.

References

68 Independent Monitoring Board of the Polio Eradication Initiative (2015) 11th Report, May. Introduction.

69 Carter, J. (1981) President Jimmy Carter's Farewell Address, January 14, 1981. *http://www.jimmycarterlibrary.gov/documents/speeches/farewell.phtml*.

70 Hare, R. (1970) *The Birth of Penicillin and the Disarming of Microbes*. George Allen and Unwin, London (p. 87).

71 Neushul, P. (1999) Fighting research: army participation in the clinical testing and mass production of penicillin during the Second World War. In *War, Medicine and Modernity*, eds Cooter, R., Harrison, M., Sturdy, S. Sutton, Stroud.

72 Milo, D. (1997) Street names. In *Realms of Memory*, ed. P. Nora, trans. Goldhammer, A. Columbia University Press, New York.

73 Smil, V. (2001) *Enriching the Earth: Fritz Haber, Carl Bosch, and the Transformation of World Food Production*. MIT Press, Cambridge, MA.

INDEX

Index

Index

Index